GOD'S TRIBESMAN

By the same authors
Christ in Bangladesh

GOD'S TRIBESMAN
The Rochunga Pudaite Story

James and Marti Hefley

A. J. HOLMAN COMPANY
Division of J. B. Lippincott Company
Philadelphia and New York

266.022
H46g

U.S. Library of Congress Cataloging in Publication Data

Hefley, James C
  God's tribesman; the Rochunga Pudaite story.

  1. Pudaite, Rochunga. I. Hefley, Marti, joint
author. II. Title.
BV3269.P8H43   266'.022'0924 ₁B₁   74-3346
ISBN-0-87981-031-9

TO
J. PAUL AND HELEN DRISCOLL,
MARTI'S SPIRITUAL PARENTS,
WHO HAD A PROMINENT PART
IN PRAYING US TOGETHER

ACKNOWLEDGMENTS

The concern for this book originated with Faith Mains, who introduced us to Rochunga Pudaite. After researching an article for *Christian Life*, we knew that Faith was right—a biography of Ro must be written.

Her husband, Doug, was just as enthusiastic and helpful. So was Joe Musser, board member of Bibles for the World, who served for a year as Vice President of Partnership Mission while on leave from his regular job as Director of Creative Projects for Fourmost Productions. Joe provided basic information and set up the first interviews. More recently, the Rev. Weyburn Johnson, Assistant to the President of Bibles for the World, helped by providing information on the mission's operation.

Our primary source was, of course, Rochunga Pudaite. Besides turning over to us his unfinished autobiographical manuscript, Ro gave us a great deal of his time. In every interview he was open and revealing, even when embarrassing subjects were pressed.

For background information on Ro we are indebted to his wife, Mawii Pudaite; his father, Chawnga (who came from India to help); and the Rev. Ruolneikhum Pakhuongte (Khuma). Americans who were especially helpful are the Rev. Earl King, Dr. Bob Pierce. Dr. Kenneth Taylor, and Dr. Carl Wenger.

7

The secretarial staff of Bibles for the World could not have been more cooperative. We thank them all, particularly Donna Kaptan, Marcia Fator, Peggy Meyer, Ruth Larson, and Donna Sewell.

Finally, we are indebted to Faye Park for careful and conscientious typing of the final manuscript and to our children, Cyndi, Celia, and Cheri, for understanding why both parents must spend so much time at their typewriters.

CONTENTS

An eight-page section of illustrations follows p. 144

GOD'S TRIBESMAN

CHAPTER 1

Jungle Treasure

The jeering laughter rolled through the crowd as the family members took up their packs. Five-year-old Rochunga indignantly kicked at the dirt outside the bamboo hut that was no longer his home.

"How dare they laugh at our father!" he said to his older brother, Ramlien. "Don't they know God wants our father to move from Senvon to Phulpui, where there is no church?"

The little, half-naked, round-faced boy saw a church elder pulling at his father's arm. "Please, Chawnga. Leave your family here. Your wife will die on this hard journey." Then Ro saw the glint in his father's dark eyes.

"We *must* go. God will help her."

His ailing mother's lips moved. "Yes, God will help me."

Ro watched his father gently take his mother's hand and lift her to a standing position. "Make way, friends," Chawnga said decisively. "The sun grows warm."

As the crowd parted before his father's determined stride, Ro reached for his mother's other hand. She had been ill for as long as he could remember. "*Chibai* [goodbye], *chibai*," he called with the rest of the family, and they were on their way.

Still smarting from the ridicule continuing around them,

Ro straightened his shoulders and pumped his short legs to
keep up. He suddenly realized that his mother's hand was
hot and damp. Peering anxiously up past her long native
skirt and wrap-around blouse, he saw that her face
glistened with perspiration. He heard her labored breathing and wondered how much farther she could go. What if
the jeering villagers were proven right?

They had walked nearly half a mile to the end of the
village when she stopped, swayed, and collapsed on the
rocky ground. "Mother, Mother, are you all right?" Ro
cried as everyone crowded around her.

"We told you so!" someone said smugly. "We knew she
couldn't make it!"

"Stand back!" he heard his father command. "Give her
air!" Ro huddled with the other children as their father
took a gourd jug and poured water on her head. Then,
heart pounding, Ro listened to his father pray. "Great
God, you have called me to far regions. Give Daii strength
to go with me. Let her *walk!*"

Ro looked at his mother. Her eyes were fluttering. She
was smiling weakly. "Let us walk on," she said. Amazed,
Ro took her hand again and pulled as his father helped her
to her feet.

At the brow of the hill they stopped and gazed across the
green jungles of northeast India. In that spring of 1932
it was a wild land, populated by fierce Bengal tigers,
pythons, roving herds of wild elephants, and strange
tribesmen hardly known in the outside world. Some of the
pessimistic villagers left the entourage here, but a few
kept following as the family pressed onward. Ten miles
they walked that day through clouds of oppressive mosquitoes and ambushes of painful bloodsucking leeches,
stopping only for brief rest periods, and when they halted
for the night at Lungthulien village, a few of the mockers
were still there to predict that Daii would not live to see the
sun rise.

Exhausted from the day's walk, Ro fell asleep to the sounds of the jungle night.

The next morning he awoke with a start in the strange hut. Pattering to Daii's bed, he called softly, "Mother, are you yet living?"

"Yes, my son." She smiled. "I am living." As if to prove how alive she was, she got up all by herself and began boiling rice for breakfast. Ro watched in awed amazement. It was the first meal he had ever seen his invalid mother prepare.

They continued on the hard journey. Along the trail Ro slipped and sprained his ankle. An uncle had to carry him to the swift Barak River, where he enjoyed being poled across on a bamboo raft.

In just three days they reached Phulpui village, where a new crowd of the curious fell in behind them. Going to the hut Chawnga had built on a previous trip, they were pleased to discover that they had arrived before their porters, who had taken a precipitous shortcut.

While Chawnga explained to their curious neighbors why they had come, the children inspected the house. It stood on stilts with a split bamboo floor, bamboo walls, and a thatched roof. The open porch (*sawngka* in the Hmar language) was for drying clothes and for relaxing and entertaining friends in the evening. Behind the *sawngka* was an enclosed veranda (*sumphuk*) where the women would pound rice and the men do small carpentry tasks. In the main room was a large raised hearth (*tap*) made of hard, kneaded earth within a wooden frame. In the center of the *tap* were three fixed stones for the cooking pots to sit upon. A few feet beyond the *tap* was the row of beds.

The porters arrived and were surprised to find Daii still alive. Ro watched proudly as his mother served tea, and then he sat still while both parents offered a prayer of thanksgiving for Daii's healing.

The climate in Phulpui was not as good as in Senvon. It

was at a lower altitude, the sun was warmer, and the mosquitoes thicker at night. But such minor discomforts didn't stop Ro's father from building a bamboo church on a plot which the chief assigned at the far edge of the village. Chawnga had wanted the church to be in the center of the community, but the chief said there were too few Christians for that.

The Sunday for their first services in the little ten- by fifteen-foot building was a special day. Ro and Ramlien washed their faces and slicked down their hair and pulled on shirts and shorts. Before leaving the house, Ro peered into the big black pot on the front porch. The clear water reflected his smiling face. He did look grand!

As they marched proudly along the road to the church, he was conscious that the village boys were looking them over—admiringly, he felt. Then he heard laughs and giggles and a shrill voice saying, "They let the cows lick their heads!"

Ro was so chagrined he immediately messed his hair and rushed on to the church. "What happened to your hair?" his father demanded. When the downcast youngster explained, his father said, "Go comb it again. You will look fine."

The service began with only the preacher's family and two others present. However, Chawnga thundered his message as though a thousand people were there. With only bamboo walls to shut out the sound, most of the villagers heard him clearly in their homes. Ro grinned; the chief hadn't known what a powerful voice his father had.

"Over a hundred years ago," his father said, "a Hmar wise man foretold the coming of white-skinned people who would load guns from the bottom. They came and conquered our land. This same wise man said the bottom loaders would be followed by others telling us of a new religion not requiring sacrifice of animals or chickens.

"This new religion was brought first to Senvon, from

which my family and I came. We have now come to tell
you about the true trail to God. Follow this trail and you
will know forgiveness for your evil deeds and happiness for
living. Listen to what God's Word says. . . ."

By delivering such sermons and visiting every home in
the village, Chawnga had a sizable congregation by Christmas. Ro was glad, for this meant an exciting time at the
feast. While the Hmar Christians did not celebrate birthdays (Ro knew the date he was born only because his
father had written it down; most Hmars were not so
fortunate), Christmas was a big occasion.

On Christmas morning the Christians came, bringing
their gifts to Jesus. After the service, they gathered outside for the gifts to be distributed to widows, orphans, and
other needy people. Then came singing, games, and a community feast of roast pig and wild buffalo boiled in a huge
pot that took two men to carry. Though Ro did not receive
any gifts, it was the nicest time of the year for him.

After the second year, with the church having been enlarged twice, Chawnga began spending more time preaching in the other twenty villages in the Vangai range for
which he was responsible. Sometimes Daii would accompany him while her mother and two aunts cared for the
children.

Frequently they brought home orphans, whom they
treated as members of the family. Still, Chawnga always
had time to help his sons make traps or take them fishing.
And before bedtime they often had a story.

So it was natural for Ro to ask one evening on the
sawngka, "My father, who first told you of the gospel?"

Chawnga smiled, for he never tired of telling stories.
"Well, my son," he began—Hmars seldom called each
other by name—"when I was young, a friend, Hluonte,
and I walked six days to the Lushai village of Aijal. We
hoped to sell some chickens and make a profit. Along a

street we met three strange white men. Two had reddish
brown hair and eyes blue like the sky.

"They said they were missionaries. They promised to
buy our chickens for a fair price if we would follow them
to their mission home. We did, and they kept their word.

"Hluonte and I called the oldest Mr. Old White Man,
the second, Mr. Other White Man, and the third, Mr.
Young White Man. Mr. Young Man told us he had come to
India from a land called Wales the year before the flower-
ing of the bamboo [1908]. He said his name was Watkin
Roberts.

"Mr. Young Man was kind to us. He didn't seem as
foreign as the others, for his hair was black like ours. He
told us of God's Son, who he said had died as a sacrifice for
our sins.

"He talked to us a long time about believing in God's
Son and taking his ways as our own. I liked what he said,
for I knew the ways of our tribe were bad. My father—
your grandfather—took heads and hung them proudly on
his house. I did not think sacrifices could forgive such sins.

"But I could not accept Christianity then. I knew our
people would turn from me if I did not sacrifice. The
priest would not help me when I was sick. The young
people would not invite me to their parties; Mr. Young
Man said a Christian did not drink rice beer.

"There was something else. Mr. Young Man said Christians counted days in units of seven, instead of counting the
days of the moon as we did. The first of those seven days
was to be a rest day, when we worshiped God and did not
work. I thought if I did not go to the fields that day, people
would think I was lazy!

"I told Mr. Young Man I could not be a Christian. But I
kept thinking of what he had said and hoped he would
come to Hmar land.

"You see, in those days foreigners were afraid we would
take their heads. But that didn't stop Mr. Young Man. Why,

once when he heard that a dying Lushai chief was having his slaves buried with him, he traveled day and night to save them. The slaves were already buried to their waist when he arrived. He ordered his native helpers to dig them out, and nobody laid a hand on him."

Sitting beside his father, Ro sighed in admiration. "He must have been very brave, Father."

"He was, my son. He knew the British Agent didn't approve, but he would sneak into Hmar territory and return before dark. Finally he was invited by our Chief Kamkholun to come all the way to Senvon. The agent gave him permission but warned him he would probably be killed. Instead of killing him, the people of Senvon gave him gifts and listened respectfully to his message. I was only fifteen, but as the son of the former chief I listened carefully to Mr. Young Man and soon afterward I became a Christian.

"Mr. Young Man could stay only three days, but he promised to return if possible. The government never let him come back to us. We who became Christians had to go out to him for further training."

Chawnga stood up and stretched. "But that is another story and too much for you to understand now. It is time for all children to be in bed."

Ro lay on his mat and tried to think what it must have been like not to know about Jesus. All his life he had heard Bible stories. His mother had sung Christian songs to him as a baby. Even his name, Rochunga, meaning "God's highest treasure," had Christian significance. "My father became a Christian about the time you were born," Daii had often reminded him. "He wanted you to be named as a testimony of what he had received from God." Ro drifted off to sleep, still wondering.

When his father was away traveling, Ro's days seemed routine. He and his brother were responsible for bringing in the family cows and milking them each evening. In the hot, humid climate the lazy animals gave little milk, but they were also prized for meat. As long as they were not visited by any bears or tigers, this was an uneventful chore.

Ro liked to fish and catch wild fowl, but his real forte was setting snares for the white jungle rats that were considered a Hmar delicacy.

As he grew older, his rat catching drew an invitation to join the village gang. Anxious to prove he was no sissy, Ro helped them set snares for women carrying firewood from the jungle or water from the stream. Though his conscience bothered him, he pretended to enjoy watching a helpless woman squirming to free her feet.

The gang leader, Hmingte, demanded absolute loyalty from the members. One test was to skin live rats with their teeth while the rodents squealed in agony.

Ro knew his parents would never approve of such bizarre acts. Nor did he enjoy deceiving them, for until he joined the gang he had always tried to be a respectful and obedient son. Yet he seemed to be trapped in a web of evil from which he could not escape.

The breaking point came one day in the jungle. Hmingte commanded the gang to climb a tall tree, but as soon as they were up high he began chopping it down. When the boys begged him to stop, he threatened to chop off the feet of anyone who tried to reach the ground.

The terrified boys clutched the slender trunk desperately as it shuddered under each blow. As the final blow landed the tree arched and fell, carrying the screaming boys with it.

Ro hit the ground with a thud. He was stunned and bruised but shook himself and looked around at the others. "Tana!" he cried when he saw one of his friends lying motionless nearby. "Tana!" There was no response. Even Hmingte was frightened and feared the boy was dead.

"Don't anyone dare tell, or I'll kill you," he threatened as he ran off.

Tana moaned faintly and moved his head. He was not dead, but the scare had so shocked Ro that he decided to quit the gang.

A few days later his father returned from a trip and took Ro fishing. They walked down to the river and drained a pool so they could catch the trapped fish by hand. As Ro felt between the rocks for fish, he asked, "My father, why must you be gone so often?"

"My son, you know there are many of our people who have not yet heard that God sent his Son to die that we might have everlasting life. I must go tell them."

Ro caught a shiny *ngahra* and tossed it on the bank. I've known that all my life, he thought solemnly, but it's made no difference. I'm no better than the other boys in the gang. He flipped another fish to the bank, but his enthusiasm was gone.

After a while his father seemed to sense that something was troubling him. "Let's rest," he suggested. "The fish will not go anywhere."

They sat on the mossy bank and watched a mischievous monkey swing above them. Ro waited for his father to talk about spiritual matters, but Chawnga seemed content to just spend some time alone with his son.

Later they headed home, each carrying a string of fish. Despite his inner disquietude, Ro felt warm for having been with his father.

The next Sunday evening, after closing his sermon, Chawnga extended an evangelistic invitation. "If you truly believe and want to follow Jesus, you will not be ashamed to say so publicly," he declared.

Ro stepped to the front. "My father, I believe, and I have asked Jesus to forgive me," he announced solemnly.

"Has he?" his father queried earnestly.

Ro nodded. "If it is written in his Book that he will forgive those who ask him, then he has taken away each and every sin. God would not lie."

"It is written in his Book," Chawnga assured him.

Some days later Chawnga began to talk of a great need in the Hmar tribe. "My son, you know we do not have God's Word in our own language. We have only the Lushai Bible, and many Hmars do not understand it. Someone must write God's Word in Hmar and have copies printed for everyone."

"Can you do it, my father?" Ro asked.

Chawnga shook his head sadly. "I have not the learning. Nor does any other Hmar. And missionaries are not allowed to live with us."

A long pause stretched between them.

"How much learning would be required?" Ro finally asked.

"More than you can receive in the little school here. You would have to go away.

"You know it is the custom in our Leiri clan for the eldest son to inherit his father's property," Chawnga went on. "It will be your brother Ramlien's responsibility to take care of your mother and me. But we will not send you away against your will. You must want to have an education."

Ro sat very still. He had heard Hmars speak with awe of the knowledge of an educated man. His uncle had said if one were to finish primary school, high school, college, and then earn a master's degree, one would know *everything*. "Why, you could stand on the root of any tree and know how many leaves were hanging from its branches!" he had said.

"I think I would like to be an educated man," Ro decided solemnly.

Chawnga and Daii arranged for their son to attend the Churachandpur Mission School, ninety-six miles to the east toward Burma. Even with Ro working to pay for his board, Chawnga would have to contribute one fourth of his monthly salary.

Ro was excited until he learned how far he would have to walk through the jungle. "Look how short and puny my legs are," he said to his father.

Chawnga ran his hand up the short, brown, stocky legs and smiled. "What muscles you have! I had never noticed how strong your legs are."

Ro walked off on his "strong legs," believing the walk might not be so bad after all, but a little later he returned to his father. "Have you considered, sir, that I have only one pair of shorts?"

Chawnga chuckled. "Have confidence, my son. Your mother and I will see that you have sufficient clothing."

Then he thought of the possibility of meeting a tiger on the trail. His father had promised to walk with him the first time, but even he was no match for a Bengal tiger. When Ro confided this fear, Chawnga assured him that God would protect them.

But Ro was not so certain a few days later when he and Ramlien were driving the cattle home. They saw a reddish flash, then heard a cow bellow. Within seconds the cattle stampeded all around. And the tiger—there it stood on the far side of the road, eyeing them hungrily.

Ro tried to shout, but his voice was gone. In an instant of paralyzing fear, a verse his father had taught him came to mind: "though I walk through the valley of the shadow of death, I will fear no evil."

Suddenly he heard a man call, "Clap your hands and shout!" The boys did and the tiger loped away.

Still Ro was not completely confident. It wasn't just the long walk. He would be far from home for ten months at a stretch. He was pondering this one Sunday morning in church when his father translated a verse from the Lushai Bible that puzzled him: "having loved his own which were in the world, he loved them unto the horizon" (John 13:1).

As they walked home together, Ro said politely, "My father, that was a fine sermon . . . but there was something wrong."

"What?" Chawnga asked, stopping short.

"You said God's love is unto the horizon, but you did not tell how far the horizon is. If God loves me only as far as I can see, how can I trust him? How far is the horizon?"

"I don't know," came the quiet reply.

Ro continued his argument in the careful, respectful Asian manner. "Sir, if you talk about things you do not know, if that is what education does for you, I cannot go to school."

There was no answer.

Later he was invited by his father to hike up nearby Sumtuk mountain. When they reached the top, Chawnga said, "Let us climb this tree."

From their perch they could see a great distance. Chawnga pointed downward. "That is the Cachar Valley, where my father and other Hmars attacked the tea plantation and took five hundred heads. The smoke is from the fires that heat the leaves. It is many days' journey across that valley.

"Now look to the long mountain range beyond. Do you see the peak where the heaven kisses the earth?" He paused, waiting for Ro to respond.

"Yes, my father," Ro replied, puzzled. "But why do you ask?"

"Because," Chawnga continued, "if you were to journey many weeks and come to the top of that mountain and look, you would see another just like that one. Then if you journeyed on again for many days and weeks to the second mountain you would be able to see a third. If you were to go to the third mountain and look, you would see yet another. The horizon is never-ending, my son. There is no place in this world where the love of God has not touched or cannot reach.

"When you go to school, whether you are on a mountain or in a valley, God will encircle you with his love. He will guide you, protect you, inspire you, and refresh you. And someday you may also become a carrier of this love that reaches unto the horizon. You may be the one to put God's Word into our language."

The vivid lesson left Ro without further argument. While he was still in the tree, he committed himself in obedience to follow God unto the horizon.

CHAPTER 2

School Daze

Ro's great day came just after his tenth birthday. He had a new umbrella to ward off the scorching sun and pounding rain on the ninety-six-mile hike to the mission school. He had hidden his precious *pawis*, or elephant beans—beans that were used as containers for tiny elephants carved of ivory—in the thatched roof. His few belongings would be carried on his back in a small pack.

After a hasty breakfast, his mother read the Twenty-third Psalm from the Lushai Bible and asked the Lord's protection and guidance for their journey. Shouldering his pack, Ro received her final tearful embrace. Then, trying hard not to cry, he followed his father through the yard and along the path that led toward the jungle.

Walking single file, they had hardly been swallowed up by the thick foliage when Ro felt a twinge of homesickness. He thought of his mother, his brothers and sister, his friends, and the homemade toys he was leaving behind. His father sensed the problem and began pointing out jungle sights: a black bear snoozing by a log, two monkeys swinging from a slim bamboo, a brown turtle sunning on a rock under the pole bridge they were crossing, darting fish in the water beneath.

When they started down a long hill, Chawnga began

describing tricks Ro could use in defending himself from wild animals on future trips he would have to make alone.

"Suppose a big rogue elephant chases you. What could you do?"

Ro's eyes darted about to see if there was one in sight. "I wouldn't be able to get away," he said resignedly. "He'd pick me up by his trunk and smash me on a tree."

"Oh, you would have a chance," his father replied with a twinkle in his eye. "First, you must remember that all elephants are left-handed. So if an elephant chases you, run straight ahead, then make a sharp turn to the right, run straight again, then take another right turn. Do this four times and you will be back on your original course."

"But how will that help?"

"Because elephants are left-handed and cannot turn quickly to the right. If they try they will fall to the ground, and it takes a long time for one to get up."

Ro wasn't sure whether this trick would work or not. He hoped the opportunity would never arise to try it out.

"Something else you must remember," the tribal preacher said. "Satan is left-handed too. He is the enemy of your soul and would like nothing more than to lead a ten-year-old boy into sin. If you are tempted to evil while far from your parents, turn to the right by reading the Word of God. Tell Jesus about this rogue, and he will tumble him on his back."

They saw no elephants that first day, but they did come across fresh tiger tracks in a stream bed. They camped for the night in the shelter of a rock, and Ro fell asleep in the security of his father's prayers.

The next morning Chawnga began reminiscing about Watkin Roberts.

"Mr. Young Man was a very unusual white man. He came to India when he was only twenty-two. He had been converted in a great revival among the Welsh people and

wanted to share his faith. But he did not treat us as other
white men did. He would never demand that tribal people
be his coolies and carry his baggage without pay. When
we accompanied him, he always called us his traveling
companions. When he went by train, he would not sit in
the first-class cars while his helpers traveled third class.
No, everyone rode together. They ate together. They slept
together.

"He made us feel intelligent. He tried to understand
our ways. He trained us to spread the gospel, but he didn't
say we had to do it in foreign ways. Why, he even made
my good friend Dohunna his field secretary.

"The people loved and respected Mr. Young Man. If only
he could have stayed. . . ." Chawnga sighed wistfully.

"Why did he leave, my father?"

"I will explain another day. When you are a bit older."

They slept four more nights in the jungle. On the sixth
day Ro awoke stiff and sore. When he stood, a sharp pain
reminded him he had sprained his ankle the day before.
There were thirteen more miles to go, his father said. Six
downhill, four up and across the Hiengkawt Pass, and the
final three miles down. Ro wondered if he could make it
on his swollen feet.

After a scanty breakfast of rice and a torrid chili chut-
ney, Ro discovered that a downhill walk with a sprained
ankle and swollen feet was pure agony. He gritted his
teeth and tried not to complain while every step felt as if
he were walking in a lake of fire. He was too big to cry or
ask to be carried but too little, it seemed, for such an
arduous journey.

Chawnga knew he was suffering, and when the width of
the trail permitted he walked close to his son, sometimes
holding his hand and trying to divert his attention with
more stories.

Chawnga's interesting talk kept Ro going until they

stopped at the narrow River Turi for lunch. Ro ate while cooling his burning feet in the water. Then they crossed over and began the uphill climb along a narrow, rocky path. His feet and ankle began flaming again. Even with the umbrella the heat pressed down until his skin glistened with perspiration. As his mouth got dryer and dryer and his tongue began to feel like parched goat's hide, he wondered if school was really so important.

Three hours later they reached the end of the pass and rested in the refreshing breeze that blew from the east. After a short walk, Chawnga pointed out to Ro the shiny tin roofs of houses in the next valley. This was Churachandpur, their destination. Ro tingled with new confidence and fairly flew down the hill.

They went to the mission dispensary, where Chawnga made arrangements for Ro to lodge with a Mr. Thanglung, a young medical practitioner. The cost, he told Chawnga, would be 3 rupees (then about 45 cents) per month, plus whatever work the boy was capable of doing.

The time came for Chawnga to leave. Ro clung to his father's hand, striving to control his emotions.

"Good-bye, my son. God keep you," the tribal preacher said with strong self-will. Then he left quickly.

The Thanglungs decided that Ro was "capable" of tending their herd of thirty-five cows—milking them each morning before breakfast, taking them to their grazing ground, and then, after classes, getting them in the evening. He was also to weed the garden and help with household chores.

He envied the boys who lived in the dorm and could play soccer during their free time. With so much work, he had little time even for study.

Schoolwork was a struggle. Each teacher taught in his own native tongue, which meant the students had to know five different languages. Fortunately, Ro had heard some

of the languages on trips he had taken with his father,
or he might have given up immediately. As it was, he was
able to understand all his teachers within three months
and was soon studying English, which it was hoped would
become the common language at the school.

As soon as he was settled into the routine, Ro wrote a
letter to his parents. There were no post offices in Phulpui
or the other Hmar villages, but there were mail runners
and travelers who would take correspondence. Ro sealed
his envelope and addressed it simply to "My Father,
Phulpui Village." He would not show disrespect by using
his father's name. Then he dropped the letter into the box
for outgoing mail.

Later in the day a teacher asked the class, "Who is this
writing to My Father, Phulpui Village?" The other students tittered while Ro cringed in his seat. Humiliated, he
had to admit it was he and then listen to the teacher explain
the "proper" way to address a letter.

Despite early difficulties, the Hmar boy's confidence began to climb. He found that some of the students had heard
of his father's reputation as a fearless evangelist and strong
preacher. He became aware that because of his father he
was looked upon as a leader.

When the students elected him president of the Junior
Christian Endeavor, Ro suggested that they divide into
groups of three or four and witness in nearby villages. The
youthful gospel teams went out the next weekend with
great enthusiasm.

The village of Teisieng, six miles from the school, was
totally non-Christian. Each group that had tried to pene-
trate it reported that the people there were wild against the
gospel.

Ro knew that it was his responsibility as the leader to go,
so he asked God to protect him and started out. Before
reaching the first houses he saw priests up ahead, per-

forming ritual sacrifices, and around them villagers shouting drunkenly to one another. Suddenly the dogs began barking and squealing. Fearing he would be noticed, he stood trembling underneath an oak, wanting to run. After some indecision he dropped to his knees. "Lord, I am afraid. You gave courage to David and Joshua. Now be with me."

Standing erect, he swallowed hard and walked straight ahead. At the first home he visited, the man shouted at him, "You believers of God bring nothing but trouble. Who asked you to come here?" Ro took the hint and left.

Moving on, he stopped where three men were sitting by a fire and stood silent for several minutes. Finally gathering his courage, he asked permission to tell the story of Jesus. One man jumped to his feet. "Don't bother us with a dead man's story," he snarled. "Where is my *dao?*" And he reached for the long knife which had been used by mountain people for generations to chop bamboo, clear fields, and take heads.

Ro took to his heels with obscenities sounding behind him.

One of the men started after him. "Wait!" he shouted. "Wait!"

Ro ran as fast as his short legs would carry him, but the villager kept gaining.

"Don't be afraid. I won't hurt you," he said. Then, drawing up beside Ro, he continued, "Someone from Churachandpur has been telling me about Jesus. I want to hear more. Come to my house."

Though fearful of a trick, Ro went and shared with the stranger what his parents had taught him.

An hour later the man announced, "I want to give my name to Jesus." Ro was amazed, for this was the most explicit way he knew of declaring, "I will become a Christian." The tribespeople felt that when one gave his name to another, he was giving himself away, trusting that the recipient would prove worthy of his confidence. That was why they were always reluctant to tell their names, preferring that a friend do it for them indirectly.

Ro took a slip of paper from the Lushai New Testament he was carrying and solemnly wrote down the name of the first Christian in the village. Then, after promising to return, he returned to school rejoicing.

November vacation time came and Ro set out for home in the company of several older boys who lived in villages along the way. The first night in the jungle they were drenched by a cold rain that continued all the next day. At sundown they stopped at a village where they hoped to find shelter.

By knocking at doors, they all found places to stay except Ro. Dejected and wet, the Hmar boy sat on a cold tombstone at the edge of the village and cradled his head between his knees. "Lord, don't you love me any more?" he asked mournfully. "Will you let me pass the night hungry and cold?" Then he began to cry.

A man's voice broke into his sobs and asked why he was crying. When Ro explained, the stranger said, "I'm the chief here. It is a shame to our village that you have found no welcome. Come and be my guest for the night."

The chief even carried Ro's soaked luggage, and when they arrived at the house he commanded his servants to bring dry clothes and a hot drink to warm Ro while a meal was being prepared. Later, in a warm dry bed, Ro remembered the day he climbed the tree with his father, and he thanked God for loving him unto this horizon.

On the sixth day he reached Phulpui, tired but thrilled to see his family, which had grown to include a new brother. Everyone seemed to respect his increased status. He felt himself to be a very worldly-wise and much-traveled young man.

The excitement of revival was then stirring Phulpui. Early in the morning people were praying, raising their hands and praising God, calling for God's blessings on the tribe. There were services every night, and on Sundays each unbelieving home received four or five evangelistic visitors. Ro's father reported happily that God's power was exploding in other Hmar villages, with hundreds of tribespeople following God's trail.

Ro's curiosity about Mr. Young Man could not be held in check. "My father, why did he leave?" he asked. "Why is he not with us now?"

Chawnga stared at his growing son. "Well, I suppose you must learn sooner or later. Sit down, my son, and I will try to explain.

"Missionaries are people just like us," he began. "They don't always agree. And some become jealous of those who bring many to God. Mr. Young Man was becoming much loved by us and had obtained permission from the British Agent to work in Hmar territory. Then another missionary told the British Agent that church leaders in England and America had divided up India among various missionary groups and that he had been assigned the state of Manipur.

"This missionary felt Mr. Young Man—Watkin Roberts —should leave the southwest part of Manipur where Hmars live. Because the other missionary had a relative in the government, the British Agent cancelled Mr. Young Man's permit."

Ro was indignant. "So that's why Mr. Young Man had to leave."

"He left Manipur, but not India. He started a training school outside the state, and we went to him for training. Mr. Young Man believed that we, not foreigners, should lead our churches. He said we should use our own tunes in worship and follow our own ways so long as they were pleasing to God."

"Is he still in India?"

"No, my son. His missionary society became worried about the loyalty of tribal leaders. They wanted us to have foreign bosses. Mr. Young Man wouldn't have it that way, so they stopped his salary. An unbeliever gave him money for passage home.

"They sent in foreign bosses to tell us what to do. Some of our preachers refused to work for them and were whipped by officials. I tried to preach without any salary for a whole year but had to give up and let them pay me. What else could I do?

"Don't let this worry you, my son. We are not responsible for the mistakes of others. Remember, the missionaries are doing many good services. Without them, there would be no school at Churachandpur for you to attend."

"I know," Ro agreed. "But does Mr. Young Man yet live?"

Chawnga smiled. "Yes. He is in Canada working and raising money for missionary work in India. Some of us receive letters from him. He hopes to come back someday."

"If he does," Ro said with a gleam in his eye, "I will be the first to carry his baggage."

The two months of vacation passed too quickly and Ro had to return to school again—this time alone. Traveling by day was not so bad since he felt himself to be a big boy now. But at night the fears of the jungle haunted him.

One night he was awakened by the throaty growl of a tiger. He knew it was hopeless to run. The royal Bengal could easily catch him. He could only lie very still under the tree, listening as the jungle cat circled closer and closer until finally it was within springing distance.

What was there to do but pray? No fancy prayer with eloquent phrasing; just, "Lord I don't want to be this tiger's breakfast. Keep his mouth shut!"

The Bengal started walking away! Ro held his breath

and listened as the swish of tall grass became fainter and fainter until he was sure that the tiger had disappeared into the dark jungle. Then he thanked God for loving him unto this horizon.

School was more enjoyable for Ro the second year. He was doing well in all his subjects, except English. The words were hard to pronounce. And there were so many exceptions to the grammatical rules. But he especially liked geography, for it enlarged his view of the world.

He traced on a map how far Watkin Roberts had traveled from Wales to bring the gospel to the hill people of northeast India. And he ran his fingernail across the great Pacific Ocean along the route he thought the missionaries might have come from America.

The lands on the other side of the world continually intrigued him. What wonders must be there, he mused, as he thought of stories brought back by tribesmen who had been taken by the British to fight in the Great War a quarter century before. He had heard men tell of digging meals out of the ground, of seeing a machine with wings that actually flew, of visiting a place where steel wire grew like corn, of seeing a man shot from a giant gun into enemy territory. Former tribal soldiers had also whispered tales of the immoral conduct of Europeans, indicating that many did not follow God's ways. Ro was now mature enough to know that the stories had been embellished over the years, but he wished that one day he might go and see for himself.

The year Ro was twelve, he reminded his father of a secret desire. Chawnga was leaving for the eighty-mile walk to buy supplies at a trading post. "My father," he entreated, "if you could, if it were possible, I would like a pair of shoes."

Chawnga made no promises, but he returned with a pair

of white sneakers. Ro slipped them on his feet; they looked fine. He took them off, then tried them on again. On and off, and on and off. He felt like royalty.

Running to show his friends, he accidentally stepped in mud. His beautiful white shoes were soiled! Sadly, he hurried home and washed off the red clay and put them near the stove to dry.

Two hours later he looked and saw to his horror that the rubber had melted away from the soles. When he tried them on again, his toes stuck out. Losing all decorum, he cried. How he cried! Most of the night he sobbed, berating himself. "Your first pair of shoes, and you melt them, you stupid boy!"

Early the next morning he sought out Chawnga. "I know you spent much money, my father. I am deeply sorry for my foolishness. Could you forgive me for being so wasteful?"

"My son, I will always have as much forgiveness as you need," Chawnga replied soberly. "Let us pray about it. Lord, because of his foolishness my son has ruined his first pair of shoes. Will you forgive him? I have already done so."

Even though Ro knew it would be months before his father went again to the store, he felt better. His shoes were gone, but his heart was at peace.

Ro thought about forgiveness as he studied history the next year. So many lessons seemed to be about wars and killing. His own people had taken heads for generations. Civilized countries had fought the Great War in Europe. Now stories were coming that another war in Europe had started up.

Ro had just finished his primary schooling at Churachandpur when the Japanese invaded the subcontinent, captured Rangoon, and began marching north. He had planned to attend the American Baptist High School in Jorhat, Assam, four hundred miles from Phulpui. Now India was forced into the conflagration that had encircled the world. The Jorhat school was made a barracks for Indian troops.

Fired by patriotic fervor, Ro tried to enlist in the Indian Army. Age was no problem, since the Hmars kept no birth records. But a recruit had to be sixty inches tall and have a thirty-five-inch chest.

At fifteen he was tall enough. However, no matter how deep a breath he took or how much he swelled his chest, he couldn't manage the thirty-five-inch girth.

Though he couldn't qualify as a soldier, he still wanted to help, for the Japanese were already moving into the tribal hills. "You can be an informer for Allied Intelligence," they told him. "You can report enemy troop movements and locations and help rescue Allied prisoners."

A "bamboo telegraph" was crisscrossing the jungle. Ro was proud to beome a link in the system.

CHAPTER 3

Higher Goals

The machines of modern warfare terrified the tribal hill people. They fled from the iron monsters that clanked through villages, spewing bullets and flame. The old people ran in superstitious terror when giant shiny birds marked with the rising sun roared overhead. The young looked in curiosity but ran to hide with their elders when the bombs began falling.

The invaders established their biggest camp at the Hmar center of Sielmat and almost overran Imphal, the capital of the state of Manipur. Elsewhere, armed patrols traversing the jungle made travel unsafe. There was such danger that, after running into two armed bands of Japanese, Chawnga decided to curtail his preaching tours.

Despite their fears, the tribal people aided the Allied cause. Their communications network ran letters out of the jungle in hollowed-out bamboo, though they knew death was the penalty for being caught.

Ro belonged to this ragtag force of daredevil intelligence couriers. He also spied out Japanese hideouts and gave the locations to the Indian Army. He was always paid, according to the importance of his reports, in money or in cigarettes which he sold.

The thought came that as a mountain trader he would

have an excellent excuse for traveling through villages near the front lines. "I can scout for the Indian Army and also earn money for my education," he told his father. He was so convincing that Chawnga loaned him 100 rupees (then about $40) to get started.

He bought a supply of mountain-grown chilies which he carried on his back for four days to the market town of Lakhipur. Selling the chilies for a profit, he purchased a basket of assorted knives, razor blades, needles, clothing, and popular patent medicines to peddle in distant front-line villages.

The war had brought both destruction and soaring prices to these villages. The survivors were being paid well for services and homegrown products. In turn they were eager to buy store-bought items which Ro could supply.

In a village called Bualtang, high on a Manipur hill, he learned an interesting bit of economic psychology. A Japanese patrol had recently swept through the valley, leaving unburied, decaying bodies. As a result, dysentery and cholera were spreading.

Ro scouted around the area, since it was his first visit there, and found the people very friendly. He had in his basket a bottle of five hundred cholera pills which he had bought for 20 rupees. Because the people were in such desperate need, he decided to price the tablets five to a rupee. That would turn a good profit and not be too expensive for the customers.

At his first stop he was describing how the medicine would immediately stop "running stomachs" when he overheard a listener comment in the native Vaiphei dialect, "Too cheap to do good work. Last month I bought a tablet of quinine for two rupees, and when I swallowed it I knew it was good medicine!"

Taking the hint, Ro moved to the other end of the village and began selling pills for one rupee each. By nightfall he had dispensed 350 tablets. The next morning he sold the remainder of his stock to one man for 100 rupees and left the village with a profit of 430 rupees. He saw the good fortune as a clear sign from God that he should continue his education.

It was becoming more dangerous for the intelligence runners to travel through the mountains. As the war turned against Japan, the invaders became more fierce. Ro felt it expedient to settle down for a while and farm. He had had no experience, but he was willing to work hard.

The blooming of the yellow *vulte* marked the time each year when sites from the communally owned land were apportioned among the farmers. The farmers drew slips of paper which told the locations and sizes of their sites. Those wishing to switch for some reason could do so, leaving latecomers to take the least desirable lots. Because Ro decided late, he drew a site on the main path connecting two villages through which pigs and cattle were driven daily.

He bought an ax and a long sharp knife to clear the jungle trees and undergrowth. Then he went to work with great gusto, chopping and hacking and dragging brush into piles for burning.

For a while the strenuous exercise was exhilarating. Then it turned into pure misery. All his time on the trail hadn't conditioned him for such work. Muscles ached that he hadn't known he had as the ax felt as heavy as a log in his hands. Painful blisters bubbled on his palms and soon broke and bled. His enthusiasm wore thin and he wanted to quit, to find an easier way to earn money for his education. But the noise of neighbors felling trees rang through the jungle, and he could not bear the thought of not being able to work as hard as the others.

Shoulders and arms aching and muscles twitching uncontrollably, he dragged home from his farmland (*jhum*) at sunset. Daii met him at the doorway with a cup of refreshment. What joy! "After you have drunk your tea, my son," she said tenderly, "there is warm water for you to wash your hands and feet."

Dawn came all too quickly and the torturous cycle began again. His back, arms, and chest muscles felt as if they were being stretched on a rack. The blisters, now broken and raw, burned to the slightest touch. Since he had no file to sharpen his tools, the knife and ax became hopelessly dull.

On the eighteenth backbreaking day Ro finished clearing his plot. Then he joined the others to recuperate for a month while the brush dried. On the day appointed by the headman for burning, all the piles were set afire. The entire village stood guard to see that the flames did not spread too far.

The Hmars had a time for everything. Cotton and sesame seed were to be sown when the *ling* tree flowered, soy beans planted when the locustlike cicadas sang, rice to be dropped five lunar months from the time of the last harvest.

Ro found the sowing much faster than clearing the jungle, but the ashes made the job messy. Without shade to ward off scorching rays, the sun broiled his back. He decided to build a small *jhum* house in the center of the plot for shelter.

The appearing of the first green shoots brought a sense of accomplishment. Weeding quickly cured that. He tried a group plan with five other Hmar youths. But they liked to laugh and joke and loll around on long, long lunch breaks while the weeds kept growing. After taking his turn in each of their plots. Ro politely withdrew and resumed working alone.

He had no plans for making farming a lifework. But

since it was his job for the present, he was determined to
do his best. He went to his field every day, including
Saturdays. After weeding he would gather up the weeds
and carry them outside the plot. Then he would add more
soil around each hole of rice plants. These were extra things
which his neighbors did not do. The weeding and tending
of the young plants was a slow, tedious process and had
to be continued through good and bad weather, but he
kept at it diligently.

Sunday afternoons, Ro walked to his *jhum* just to
glimpse the growing crop. Then he crept into the little
jhum house for prayer: prayer that the war might end,
prayer for a good harvest that would provide more savings
for education, prayer for his parents and for the Hmar
churches that were suffering without leadership.

Summer mellowed into autumn, and the weeding was
done. And then, harvest time, the climax of a year's hard
labor! This was the phase of farming Ro really enjoyed.
His entire family pitched in to help harvest the rice by
hand with sickles. When all the grain was in, about forty
friends came for the threshing and the feast of roast pig
that followed.

Ro had 160 bushels of rice alone! No one had expected
so many. A neighboring farmer, with a larger plot, had
garnered only half as much. Ro thanked God and set aside
16 bushels as a tithe.

The war was grinding to an end, but there was still an
occasional Allied plane being shot down over the jungle.
Ro was always glad to help the foreign airmen who seemed
so tall and pale beside the Hmars. These were the only opportunities he had to practice his English.

At last the announcement came that the Japanese had
surrendered. Not only was the war over but the British
colonial government had freed Nehru, Gandhi, and other
Indian leaders who had been jailed for trying to make

Britain grant independence as the price for Indian support in the war. It seemed only a matter of a short time now until India would become its own master.

But the Hmar area was still a world removed from New Delhi, Bombay, and Calcutta, where the call for independence was rising toward a crescendo.

Though the Hmars were little informed of world political currents, they too wanted the British masters out. As Chawnga frequently told Ro, "We governed ourselves for hundreds of years before the British came. We can get along without them. When India is free, the missionaries who opposed Mr. Young Man and his supporters will lose their power. Then he will be able to help us. I," he added proudly, "will be the first to join him."

Ro, however, was not as concerned as his father about church and mission conflicts. More than anything else, he wanted to continue his education. He had frugally saved his money from trading and farming to pay for perhaps his first year of high school. But where would he go? And if he could ever complete high school, what about college?

He heard that some American GIs were taking Indian "land boys" back with them to the United States, where an education was supposed to be much easier to get. A traveler acquaintance explained to him the duties of a land boy. "You must polish their shoes, wash their clothes, carry their burdens, and do a little cooking. The work is not hard, they say."

Ro was willing to be anyone's servant if he could go to school. He walked five days to a depot in the state of Cachar and took a train to big, noisy Calcutta. He found the place where they were interviewing for jobs and went inside. To his consternation, he could not understand a word the American recruiter was saying. This man's English did not sound at all like what he had studied in school.

The man stood him up, then motioned for him to sit,

get up again, and turn around. Then he left Ro standing in line with other hopefuls.

For two days he stood while soldiers looked over the prospects. He tried to imagine what it would be like in magical America. He prayed to be chosen. He kept thinking, maybe I'll be next. Finally he heard a word that he understood: "No." He had been rejected.

Feeling dejected and valueless, with dragging feet he boarded the streetcar that ran by the place where he was staying and sat down beside a man reading a newspaper. Curious, he looked over the man's shoulder and tried to read the English printing. He felt so utterly ignorant. He had been unable to understand the recruiter, and now he couldn't even read the paper.

After resting, Ro decided that since he couldn't go to America he would try to enroll in the St. Lawrence High School a few blocks away. The admissions officer turned him down. "All the classes are in English," he said. "We don't think you can keep up."

Ro knew of one more possibility in Calcutta—the Salvation Army. He walked to the address and was interviewed by a hefty officer with a strong British accent. This time he understood a few words, but communication was frustrating. Finally the officer said, "We'll let you know."

It was a polite rejection, but the disappointment was just as bitter as before. He had come to Calcutta brimming with enthusiasm and had been refused three times. How could he return home and admit such defeat? How could he explain that nobody wanted him?

Sadly he made the trip home, by train, by boat, and the long wearying trek by foot. He worried over what he would say about this terrible loss of face. He grew more anxious with each passing hour.

Chawnga and Daii welcomed him with open arms, and he poured out his sorrows. After he had emptied himself, his mother said, "We prayed they would not take you. We asked God to save you from going to America so you could go to high school in India and someday translate the Bible for your own people."

Then Chawnga reminded him again of his opportunity as the second son. "You know that Ramlien, our oldest, will receive the inheritance, along with the responsibility of caring for us in our old age. You are free to get the education that will fit you for the task of translation. Our people need it so badly. We know that with God's help you can do it."

Ro swallowed hard and looked solemnly at his parents. They had such great expectations for him. It seemed that by this recent bitter failure the Lord was guiding him toward higher goals. "My dear mother and father," he said with determination, "I *will* translate the Bible for our people."

CHAPTER 4

Never Give Up

Fired with the impetuosity of youth, Ro was eager to start high school. That it was too late in the year to start at Jorhat, the school in distant Assam state he wanted to attend, thwarted him not in the least. He would find another school and not lose the time.

He decided to attend a junior high school in the hill village of Lungthulien, right in Manipur. This school had been set up as a stopgap by his old friend Mr. Thanglung to meet the emergency situation created by the war.

The school year was half over when Ro presented himself to the man he had boarded with at Churachandpur before the war had stopped his education. Mr. Thanglung greeted him kindly but warned, "You'll be wasting your money. You couldn't possibly pass the year-end examination in November. If I were you I would pack my bags and go home and wait until next year."

But Ro was determined. "I would rather try and fail, sir, than not try at all," he declared. He paid his tuition and began classes the next day.

To further complicate the tribal boy's life, there was no dorm, so he had to stay with a family in the village. They lived in a large one-room bamboo house with a fireplace at one end. Despite the choking smoke, it was often necessary to huddle near the fire for warmth. And there was hardly enough room to spread his bedroll in the floor space assigned him and four other students.

Living with such a crowd in one large room made study difficult. A steady stream of visitors made concentration impossible. Ro's solution was to build himself a tree house in the jungle nearby. When heavy rain and darkness drove him from this haven, he took his books to the back porch and read aloud to offset the noise from inside.

The villagers were extremely friendly—especially the young girls. Even though he was now eighteen, a marriageable age for most Hmars, Ro feared romantic entanglement. He had resolved not to marry or have a steady girl until he had earned his college degree.

One Saturday he returned from weeding in his host's mountain farm to find all his shirts, bed sheets, and trousers nicely washed, pressed, and folded. He swallowed hard. This was the traditional Hmar way by which a village girl expressed her deep interest in a boy.

He was in a quandary. The girl would take appreciation as encouragement. He didn't want that. Yet he hesitated to soil the clothes and rewash them, which was the prescribed way of indicating displeasure. That would be insulting.

Retreating to the back porch, Ro prayed fervently that God would protect him from any girl friend. He felt his destiny was in the balance. But how could he escape such a predicament?

When he rejoined his roommates, he noticed that they seemed to be enjoying his discomfort, so much so that he became suspicious. Sure enough, Buka, the class comedian, had devised the plot. He had persuaded two young girls who liked Ro to wash the clothes and had included some of his own.

Week after week Ro studied diligently. With only one teacher who had only a high school education, many of his questions went unanswered. For the most part he had to learn on his own. He memorized most of the geometry textbook, both theorems and problems, without instruction.

When time came for the final exam that was to determine if he would get credit for a year's work, Ro was both anxious and fearful. He had tried his very best; now he could only trust God to help him recall the material he had studied.

The results were announced. He had finished third in a class of twenty-eight! He hurried to the church and offered a prayer of joy and thanksgiving to the Lord.

The next day Ro prepared for the journey back home. He took a sampan part of the way; then he began a two-day walk on a very narrow trail that included a stretch of a mile or two where the river itself was the only trail. Near the river he saw the fresh footprint of a deer. A few moments later he saw the footprint of a tiger, as well as a tiger stool that was still steaming warm. The royal Bengal had to be close by. It probably had spotted him.

He decided to go on, trying to convince himself that the tiger would be more apt to attack if he were retreating than if he advanced bravely.

As he walked along he saw more footprints. About a six-footer, he thought. Quite a big fellow.

Then, leaving the river, he heard a noise about 100 yards to his left. The tiger! He saw a reddish streak on the flashing body. There was no way of turning back now, so he continued slowly, smoothly, making no sudden motions.

He could see the tall grass moving as the tiger walked along parallel to him. Once he turned his eyes and caught a glimpse of the huge cat, but he was too scared to look any more. He kept walking . . . walking . . . a little more confidently now.

For five miles, from the river to the next village, the tiger remained with him. As he neared the village the tiger

NEVER GIVE UP 49

turned back. Ro felt like telling him good-bye, for he had come to feel the Lord must have sent that tiger for a reason. Perhaps there was some greater danger in the jungle, and the tiger was sent as my bodyguard, he thought. Certainly no other jungle animal would attack me while he was near. "Thank you, Lord, for your protection."

Chawnga and Daii were happy to learn of their industrious son's achievement in finishing a year's schoolwork in half the time. Daii had grown some red-hot chilies in her garden and was drying them to sell. Ro suggested he carry the chilies down the mountain to Lakhipur, a four-day journey, so he could sell them for a higher profit.

He struck out for the valley with sixty pounds of chilies yoked to his back. He sold the chilies for double profit and bought merchandise to sell in small villages before Christmas. These added profits were set aside for his next year of high school.

He left for the American Baptist High School in Jorhat, Assam, in January, 1946. Since the 400-mile trip was new and so far, he left home early. He was intent on not missing a day of school this year.

Traveling on foot and by bus and third-class railway coach, he reached the school a full two weeks before the semester began and asked the one resident missionary on hand for a job.

Miss Johnstone took him to a small mountain of dirt and said crisply, "You can fill in the trenches around the compound. With the war over they won't be needed."

Ro offered to contract for the job in the tribal way, so much for each trench filled. But Miss Johnstone insisted that he work by the hour. "Any time not spent working will be deducted from your pay," she told him.

He thought this a peculiar system but was challenged to see if he could work eight hours straight without stopping to rest, eat, or even drink. The next morning after breakfast he attacked the mountain—filling a basket with dirt which he carried balanced on his head for three blocks to dump in a trench. It was hard, exhausting work, and Ro was bone tired by noon.

He allowed himself only one treat during the regimen of endurance. One evening he saw his first motion picture, *Tarzan*. He was fascinated with the pictures that moved. He also thought that the United States had very unusual jungles, with vines hanging loose instead of being entwined.

At the end of two weeks the mountain was gone and eight trenches were full. Ro received his pay—just enough to pay for his meals during the period he had worked.

When classes began he accepted a new job, dorm sweeper. This menial task holds the lowest status in India, but he needed the work. Before sweeping, Ro had to walk half a mile to get water to sprinkle down the mud floor. He spent one to two hours a day sweeping and cleaning, but at least this was a contract job. He was paid about three cents a day.

Ro did well in all his classes except one. English was still his downfall. What he had learned at Churachandpur was more a hindrance than a help. He thought "whole" was pronounced "who'll," and "floor," "floo'l.' The problem was that he had been taught by people who couldn't speak the language.

He took the dictionary and tried memorizing words. But try as he would, he kept tangling up sentence structure.

English was so different from his mother tongue. In Hmar there are no masculine and feminine pronouns. The noun subject always comes before the predicate. Ro kept wanting to say, "Rice, did you eat it?" instead of, "Did you eat your rice?" In Hmar the adjectives are placed differently. He would say "the dress, pretty and red," not "the pretty red dress."

He struggled until his brain ached. He tried to speak English at every opportunity but kept stumbling with his tongue. He knew he had no chance of going to college without English, yet he feared he would never learn the language.

The missionary and national teachers at Jorhat put great emphasis on knowing English, which they hoped would become common to the twenty language groups attending the school. The prayer meetings each evening were always conducted in this foreign language.

The moment came that Ro had long dreaded. He was called upon to lead in prayer. He rose, trembling. "Our Heavenly Father . . . ," he began, and his mind went blank. He couldn't think of a single English word. He stood there in embarrassed silence, clutching the back of the pew in front of him. He could hear his friends beginning to giggle. After six or seven minutes of tortured silence the leader said a loud "Amen."

Ro slumped into his seat and buried his head between his knees, utterly ashamed and frustrated. When they were dismissed he cut study hall and ran to his dormitory bed. Irang, the dorm "father," came to see what was wrong. "Rochunga, why aren't you observing Study Hour?"

Ro pretended not to hear.

"Rochunga, are you sick?"

Ro nodded his head under the sheet and replied faintly, "I am a little sick."

Irang then put his hand on the Hmar youth and prayed, "Lord, make this boy well. He needs to know a little English. Help him. In Jesus' name, amen."

Ro pretended to be asleep when his roommates returned later, but he slept little that night. He wet his pillow with his tears as he agonized in prayer. "Lord, have you forsaken me? How can I face my friends?"

He considered packing his bag and running away before

dawn, but while kneeling by his bed he felt the touch of a hand. A voice seemed to say, *I love you. You must stay here. I will be with you. I have more things to teach you.* A sweet calm came over him, and he knew he would stay and continue to try.

After finishing his sweeping chores the next morning Ro went to the mission bungalow and borrowed the English *Book of Common Prayer* and *A Book of Prayers for the Armed Forces.* Within two weeks he had memorized nearly every prayer in the books. The English language, which had been hidden to him for so long, began unfolding for him. The humiliation in prayer meeting had driven him to just the right source of victory over the barrier that could have kept him from attaining his goal.

Near the end of Ro's first year at Jorhat, Principal J. W. Cook returned from furlough. This big, humble, spiritual man helped change the distorted image the young tribesman had of missionaries. Except for the legendary Watkin Roberts (Mr. Young Man), whom he had never seen, Ro had thought all missionaries lived in luxurious bungalows with many servants, took long naps each afternoon, strolled leisurely in the evening, and preached weekly sermons.

Dr. Cook, Ro noted, was always busy. He preached, taught, wrote, sang, visited, prayed, played, painted his house, mowed the lawn—everything. And yet he was always available and friendly and kind to the students. Ro dearly loved the huge, affable headmaster.

Ro's view of missionaries brightened even more his second year at the mission high school. Plagued by dysentery, he was twice admitted to the mission hospital, for a month each time. Knowing that the dehydrating effects of dysentery resulted in death for many tribespeople, a missionary couple, Dr. and Mrs. Frank Curry, had special meals prepared in their home for the Hmar boy, using less spices.

The nutritive, less irritating food, along with the tender loving care it represented, did the trick, and Ro returned to full health and vigor.

The civil disobedience campaign initiated in India years before was now coming to full fruition. The British offered liberty, provided the Hindu-dominated Congress and the Muslim League could reach a peaceful settlement. The decision was finally made, after much debate and bloodshed, to partition Britain's largest colony into two independent nations. The Hindu majority continued to be called India and the Muslim-dominated areas became Pakistan.

Independence Day in August, 1947, was celebrated wildly at Jorhat. As the students listened to Nehru speak, they shouted and jumped about. They heard the new prime minister appeal for peace and order. "The British ruled us yesterday, but today is in our hands. Our maturity as a nation will be demonstrated by the way we treat our British guests."

Back in Hmar land there was double reason for rejoicing. Pictures of Nehru, Gandhi, and other freedom leaders were paraded on sticks along village streets to herald their nation's political independence. The second reason for Hmar jubilation was that the old British edict that had restricted the religious freedom of the Hmar Christians was now defunct.

The tribal peoples were generally either pagan animists or Christians. Thus they did not experience the bloody religious riots that were convulsing border areas, where Hindus and Muslims were jockeying for control or fleeing to the safety of their respective majorities. Gandhi was assassinated while trying to bring peace in Bengal. Had his killer been a Muslim instead of a Hindu fanatic, a retaliatory bloodbath might have ensued.

Upon returning for his senior year, Ro was appointed

Cleanliness Supervisor by Dr. Cook. Instead of just sweeping floors, he was now responsible for seeing that the dorm and the dining room were kept clean at all times.

Despite the impressive title, the job was not enjoyable; the students didn't appreciate his reminders to clean up after themselves. Some complained that the job was too easy for the money—four whole cents a day just for walking around with pencil and paper, noting what needed to be done.

Chuba, a non-Christian student from the Ao Naga tribe, seemed to resent Ro the most. The big short-tempered soccer player deliberately smeared crumbs and rice around after each meal.

Ro explained that the mess attracted flies, which in turn would spread dysentery and diarrhea among the students, and asked everyone to please cooperate. But Chuba continued to make messes.

Then the kitchen sweepers complained about the extra work and asked Ro to stop the intentional littering or tell Dr. Cook. At the next meal Ro approached the strapping athlete and asked politely, "Are you the one?"

Chuba stood up and pushed out his chest. "Yes," he declared arrogantly. "And I am stronger than you! You are nothing. *Sala!*" he snarled, using the Assamese expression of high contempt.

"Well, the sweepers refuse to clean up your mess. You had better clean it up yourself, or I shall have to report you to Dr. Cook." And Ro drew himself up to his full five feet two.

"Report me!" the Ao Naga boy exploded. "Do it and I will kill you," he threatened, following with every filthy word he could muster.

A crowd began gathering. The other Ao Naga students spoke to one another in their own dialect, which Ro could not understand. But he sensed their intent. They wanted

to know what had happened to make their fellow tribesman angry.

Their questions suddenly turned to shouts and jeers.
They were moving toward Ro when a friend pulled him
away just in time and took him to his room.

That evening over fifty Ao Naga students were absent
from the scheduled prayer meeting. Ro returned to his
dorm to find a sign nailed to the door announcing,
"ROCHUNGA, TONIGHT YOUR HEAD WILL BE
CUT OFF!" Above the threat was a crude drawing of a
human head and beneath it the picture of a long Naga *dao*.

With several students watching, Ro removed the poster
and carried it to his room. Placing it on his bed, he knelt
and prayed. "Lord, what shall I do? I fear they mean to
do this. What shall I do, Lord?"

A voice spoke to his heart. *Trust in me. You need only
my protection.*

Within minutes Ro's friends from Manipur were in his
room. The tribal students, who were just a generation from
head-hunting, were drawing sides. The air breathed tenseness.

"We have *daos*," one of his friends said. "Let's ambush
them. Half will be dead before they know what happened!"

"No," Ro replied calmly. "Eight cannot win against
fifty. Besides, God does not have us show his love by
killing."

"Well, at least permit us to stay the night in your room
so we can protect you," another insisted.

"No, that would break the dorm rules," Ro replied. "But
before you leave, I would like you to join me in prayer."

The Manipur students stood around as Ro prayed. He
prayed particularly for the Ao Naga boys, that God would
touch their lives, that his best might be accomplished in
everyone. Then his friends left.

It was after midnight when he lay down to sleep. He
could feel his heart thumping, and his chest was wet with

sweat. He thought about the unlocked door. A stray dog
barked in a field nearby. The waning moon rose in the
east casting a faint light across the room.

Unable to sleep, he got up and lit a candle, which would
not violate the "lights out" rule. He opened his New Testament at random and began reading:

> Yea doubtless, and I count all things but loss for the
> excellency of the knowledge of Christ Jesus my Lord:
> for whom I have suffered the loss of all things, and do
> count them but dung, that I may win Christ. And be
> found in him, not having mine own righteousness,
> which is of the law, but that which is through the faith
> of Christ, the righteousness which is of God by faith:
> that I may know him, and the power of his resurrec-
> tion, and the fellowship of his sufferings, being made
> conformable unto his death; if by any means I might
> attain unto the resurrection of the dead.
>
> —Philippians 3:8–11

As he read, two phrases leaped from the page: "the
power of his resurrection" and "the resurrection of the
dead."

Again he prayed. "Lord, if the Ao Nagas are going to
cut off my head, let them do it swiftly and completely.
Don't let them just seriously wound me. But if you are
going to protect me, please give me sleep."

He lay down and within seconds fell into a deep sleep.
The next morning he awoke fully refreshed. A Manipur
boy came and said, "They will not come now. I was up all
night, and I heard them come and then move away again.
More than once they came. Did you sleep all the time?
Were you not afraid?"

"My friend, Jesus took over for me last night."

Soon Dr. Cook came. He had gotten a report. He asked

Ro to come to his bungalow, where they knelt down and he implored, "Lord, give us victory! Lord, give us victory!"

Later Dr. Cook called in the Ao Naga students. They spent long hours talking things over. Two days later, two of the leaders and Chuba came to Ro at the close of prayer meeting. They confessed they had gone to his room several times, intending to cut off his head, but something had stopped them. One kissed him on the neck and the other on the cheek. They both wept and asked for forgiveness. Chuba was sincerely repentant as he sobbed, "I am sorry."

Ro was humbled by the manifestation of "the power of his resurrection," as demonstrated in the changed attitudes of his former enemies, and his heart was filled with a surpassing love for these boys.

Soon after this experience Ro successfully passed the university high school examination which qualified him for further education. He left the mission high school at Jorhat, but his love for the Nagas would never fade.

CHAPTER 5

Testings and Triumphs

Ro was penniless after paying his final high school bills. How would he manage 100 rupees a month at St. Paul's College in Calcutta?

"I have a little savings," his father said, and pulled some bills from a hiding place.

Speechless, Ro counted out 150 rupees. This represented five months' salary for his father. With such confidence and faith behind him, surely he would make it.

After traveling four days on foot and four more by train, the Hmar youth arrived almost exhausted at bustling Sealdah station. He had prayed earnestly that his second trip to the city Kipling had called "the city of dreadful night" would not also end in failure. For an education he could stand the stench and noise and outstretched arms of the hordes of pushy beggars.

Even before the train halted, eager porters were crawling through the compartment windows. One grabbed his bedroll and walked off. When Ro caught up, the man snatched his suitcase too and rushed outside.

Ro emerged to see his baggage already on a tonga. "Where are you going?" the driver demanded.

"St. Paul's College," Ro replied.

"Fifty rupees," the man snapped.

Ro pulled his suitcase from the tonga, saying, "I can't afford that." He was walking away when the driver and an accomplice grabbed him and pulled him bodily back to the vehicle. They hurled such explicit and terrifying threats that Ro felt he had no choice but to pay the extortion: one third of his funds.

The next difficulty came when the registrar insisted he write his last name on the form. "I am Rochunga from the Leiri clan of the Hmars," Ro said proudly. "That was enough in high school."

"It is not sufficient here. We must have a last name."

Ro thought for a while and picked the name of a famous ancestor. He wrote Pudaite, meaning "descendants of Pudai."

"You should have it registered," the school official said and told him how to do it.

The first month's fees almost depleted his funds. He was willing, even eager to work, but in impoverished Calcutta there were ten applicants for each position. He wrote his father, and Chawnga borrowed 100 rupees from relatives for the next month's education.

Before that month ended, Ro applied for a scholarship available to "backward classes and tribal peoples." The application was turned down because the Hmars were not on the national census list.

Ro then wrote directly to Prime Minister Jawaharlal Nehru in New Delhi. "I am a tribal born in tribal territory of tribal parents." he stated. "I cannot understand why I do not qualify for a scholarship."

The scholarship was granted, but it was only a partial one. To earn the rest, he became a middleman for mountain traders coming to Calcutta. He met them at the station, took them to a hotel, and then took them shopping for merchandise he had already selected and bargained for. He handled all the shipping arrangements and, if they wished, threw in a tour of the city. For these services he charged one percent of every rupee spent, plus lunch and carfare. By taking only two groups a month, and with each group spending a minimum of 10,000 rupees, he earned good money—so much that he had to fight the temptation to leave college and enter business full time.

The weekly Youth for Christ rallies helped keep his sight focused on his long-range goal. The twenty-four-year-old Ro was a booster and regular participant in these rallies, the largest in Asia, which attracted from 100 to 1,000 young people. When the director, Richard Riley, talked of branching out, Ro said, "The capital of my home state of Manipur has never had an evangelistic service. Why don't we hold a rally there?"

The adventurous young American agreed, and Ro flew ahead to the city of Imphal. Except for an earlier flight from Manipur to Calcutta in a freight plane, it was his first plane trip. About half an hour before landing, one engine stopped and the other began sputtering. As the plane shook and swayed, passengers cried out in fear. Ro felt sure they were going to hit a mountain when he noticed two babies crawling around, separated from their parents.

He grabbed the babies and held them in his lap. For twenty more terrible minutes it seemed each bump or dip would be the last. Finally they made a forced landing near the Imphal airport, and passengers and crew leaped to the ground.

Ro emerged last, still holding the babies. The Hindu and Muslim passengers swarmed around him. "Your god must be very, very wonderful!" one of them exclaimed.

Riley came in on another flight and they held the services as planned, with five conversions.

Back in Calcutta, Ro entertained Frank Benson, a visiting official from the mission which had deposed Watkin Roberts. He paid the American's airport tax and then, because it was his first visit, took him sightseeing and treated him to ice cream. (Ro felt it best not to mention Watkin Roberts, since Mr. Benson was officially his father's boss.)

This contact led to Ro's being hired during his college vacation to inspect the mission's schools, which operated on a different time schedule. He traveled all summer in Manipur, visiting the schools and conferring with teachers during the day and speaking in the churches at night. He saw how children were still walking many days' journey for their education because there were no schools in their villages.

It was a significant summer for Ro. For the first time he became well known to tribal leaders, not just as Chawnga's son but as Rochunga of the Leiri clan.

In his second year at St. Paul's College, Ro spent less time on extracurricular interests and put more effort into his studies: English literature, ancient and modern history, economics, geography, and an extra English language course for further improvement. He knew he had to pass the upcoming Intermediate Arts (I.A.) examination in order to continue working toward his B.A. at a university.

After taking the exam in April, he returned to Hmar land and waited confidently for the results to be announced in June. Feeling that the best thing to do was to earn money for his next year's education, he and a cousin, Ringa, teamed up to sell a ton of dried hot chilies.

Loading the chilies aboard a rented boat, they began rowing down the rising Barak River toward Lakhipur.

As they approached their destination, the river was wild and running at flood stage. The tropical darkness was fast descending when one of the top baskets caught on an overhanging bamboo, causing the boat to lurch and almost capsize in the swirling white water.

The roaring current pulled them into the middle of the

flood. Straining every muscle, they fought to bring the boat back toward the shore. Suddenly the boat lurched again and smashed into a larger boat. The prow ran aground and water swamped the rear end. Ro pushed desperately to get his end back into deep water before everything submerged. The small boat wobbled uncertainly, then stabilized.

Too exhausted to fight the current any longer, they tied up for the night. When dawn came and they could inspect the cargo, they found many of the chilies were soaked. When they finally got the damaged goods to market, they had to be satisfied with half price.

Ro's discouragement was lightened by his high hopes as he walked to the telegraph office to pick up the results of his I.A. exam. There he read in shocked disbelief, REGRET YOU ARE UNSUCCESSFUL. He felt as if he had been kicked in the stomach. "*Un*successful!"

Tears stung his eyes. He had already applied to the famous Allahabad University for completion of his B.A. He had a government scholarship. Now it seemed his whole future had faded.

"Do you hate me, God?" he cried in despair. "Is there no more mercy left for me?"

Finally a gentle voice spoke to his heart. *I love you, Ro. You must first suffer the cross before you can enjoy the crown. Go back to Calcutta.*

"Back to Calcutta? Back to the scene of my failure? How can I, Lord?"

You have more to learn of me before you go on, the inner voice whispered reassuringly.

Reluctantly Ro went back to his parents to discuss his future. Both Chawnga and Daii agreed that he should return and repeat the I.A. course.

"There will be no scholarship," he told them, "and I have broken connections with the mountain traders. It isn't possible."

Daii looked at him with tender determination. "I will have a *jhum* this year so we will not need to buy rice," she declared. "I will grow chilies, ginger, and turmeric to sell. We will send you all your father's salary. My hands will take the hoe until you receive your B.A. degree!"

With such sacrifices from his parents, what could he do but go back?

Returning to the St. Paul's campus in July, 1951, was like carrying a knife in his heart. Eyes downcast, Ro tried to avoid other students as he walked across the campus. He felt even worse upon discovering he had failed only one subject by one point—and this the English course that hadn't been required.

If this was the sole reason for failing, why shouldn't the scholarship be renewed? he reasoned. He took his exam report to the scholarship committee, and they gave him another chance.

What a relief to know his mother would not have to work so hard. Now he was certain the Lord had some special things in store during the make-up year.

A few days later a leather-bound reference Bible arrived in the mail from an unknown donor. The inscription read: "From a friend in America who loves the Lord and the people of India."

Ro read it from Genesis to Revelation. Then again. And again. His English improved, and he found new power and endurance. He was also inspired to start translating into Hmar. Because he was repeating school subjects, he had more time. It seemed logical to begin with the Gospel of John, which Watkin Roberts had sent to the Hmars in Lushai forty-one years before.

Ro was then attending Carey Baptist Church, named in memory of William Carey, the great missionary Bible translator. A few weeks later he heard at the church a visiting American speaker from Youth for Christ who impressed him tremendously. Bob Pierce recounted experiences of preaching in China before that populous nation had fallen under Communist control. He told of refugees, war orphans, and the hunger of peoples who had never heard the name of Jesus. Afterward Ro met Pierce briefly; then the visitor had to leave for another engagement. But the American's concern for the suffering masses of Asia had spread to the Hmar youth.

All things considered, the extra year in Calcutta was very profitable—not financially, but in dedication, obedience, and spiritual maturity. When the I.A. exam was given he did well. He would be going to Allahabad.

Allahabad in the northern state of Uttar Pradesh was different from Calcutta. It was hot but not humid. The city was spacious, not congested. Everyone spoke Hindi, not Bengali as in Calcutta.

At the university dorm Ro was treated royally. Servants swept his floor, made his bed, filled his drinking water jug, polished his shoes, and even spread his mosquito nets at night. It was a strange new world to the young tribesman.

Of the 5,000 students at Allahabad there were only twenty-two Christians. They had formed a Student Christian Movement (SCM) which Ro attended. At the first meeting he suggested they make evangelism the keynote of their activities. The proposal was quickly rejected; the others wanted only social life and fellowship. "If you are a fanatic who insults others by preaching Christianity, you will walk a lonely road here," Ro was warned.

His "lonely road" began the next day when he went from door to door in the dorm handing out tracts. Some students took them politely, but others destroyed them in his presence. A few shouted obscenities. "White missionary's stool!" one shouted. Another yelled that he was "a devil for the white colonial power that has just left our country." They seemed convinced that he was part of the "white man's conspiracy."

Changing tactics, he invited students to his room to hear of his experience with Christ. Many came to debate or discuss.

His next test of faith came in the classroom. At first he felt qualified to debate with the Hindu and Muslim professors, but he soon learned they were very intelligent. They knew their arguments better than he knew the Bible.

His teacher in comparative religions termed Christianity a "topsy-turvy religion where God seeks after man. The truth is, man seeks after God," the professor declared. "Man needs a god to believe in, so he has conveniently created one. God need not seek, if he is God! That's where Christianity is wrong."

Confused, Ro went to the library. But the more philosophers he read, the more logical the teacher's argument appeared. Hume, Descartes, Spinoza, Voltaire, Bertrand Russell, and Indian philosophers left him completely bewildered.

Alone in his room, Ro studied the Bible, only to discover his teacher was right about the Judeo-Christian God. He was the "seeker," from Genesis to Revelation. The professor's words rang in his ears: "God need not seek, if he is God."

Haunted by the question, "Why does God seek after man?" Ro sat in his classes like a dumb statue. His intellectual knowledge of God had been tried and found wanting.

Sometime later he lost a pen with his initial R carved on it. He knew if he saw it he would recognize it. He searched for the pen off and on for a week; then, while returning from a sports meet, he happened to look under a hedge where he had once recovered a shuttlecock during a badminton game. There was his pen with the big R on it.

The thought came: Why have I been seeking this pen? The answer was obvious: It is my pen. I bought it, even initialed it. The pen didn't seek me. I the buyer, the owner, sought it.

The correlation—the answer to his philosophical quandary—was obvious. Of course God is the seeker! He created man, but man ran away from the presence of God. It was man that was lost, and just as I searched for the pen that was mine, God seeks those he has created, those who are lost.

His theological uncertainties evaporated like a mountain mist in the golden sunlight.

More assured and mature, he returned to the hill country after his junior year. During his short vacation he taught in a small private school for 50 rupees a month. As an upcoming university senior, he was the best-educated member of the faculty.

That fall, 1953, Ro was a dignified senior when the Congress Party's Working Committee met at the Allahabad residence of the prime minister. Ro had long wanted to inform Nehru personally about his tribe, for he feared that, if government recognition and help was not forthcoming, some Hmars might become involved in rebel activities.

He tried phoning for an appointment, but when he finally got through a no-nonsense voice said, "Sorry, you must hang up. We have too many important calls."

Not to be deterred, he donned his best suit and tie, walked over, and asked the guard at the gate how to get an appointment. The guard assured him it was impossible.

He tried a different tack. Removing the suit, he wrapped the Hmar horizontal-striped tribal cloth around his body. Then he threw another cloth over his shoulders and wiggled his feet into open-toed sandals.

Striding purposefully back to Nehru's residence, he

found a new guard on duty. "I have come from the hills of Manipur to see the prime minister," he announced confidently.

"I'm sorry, sir, but you will need a permit," the guard replied politely. Ro was about to ask how to get one when Lal Bahadur Shastri, a cabinet member, came walking across the road. "That gentleman can tell you how," the guard said, indicating Mr. Shastri.

Ro greeted the cabinet member and announced his mission. "Mr. Nehru is taking a short rest," Shastri noted. "Would you like to see his daughter, Indira Gandhi?" Ro eagerly agreed and was ushered to a porch where she was sitting.

The charming lady listened intently as he told about his large tribe that was not listed on the official census papers. She showed astonishment when he pointed out that in the 4,000 square miles inhabited by the Hmars and kindred tribes there was not a single government school or post office.

Forty-five minutes later she asked, "Do you have any of this information in writing?"

When Ro assured her that he did, she said, "You must see my father," and led him inside. Mr. Nehru was just coming out of his bedroom, but he remained a few minutes longer and took the four typewritten pages Ro had compiled.

"I will read your paper," Nehru promised. "Will you be coming to New Delhi?"

"I will come if I am needed," Ro replied.

Ro felt a new sense of destiny as he strode across the campus to the dorm. He thanked God for the opportunity and prayed that the prime minister would act.

At the moment he felt that his studies and the translation were most important. He kept translating in his spare time, concentrating on the Gospels. When his church had a study in prophecy, he did Jonah and Micah, utilizing what he learned in the course.

Everything was going well. The year 1953 ended. Then, a few days into January, he awoke with severe stomach pains. He went to a doctor and heard the frightening diagnosis of acute appendicitis. "You must have surgery, at once!" the doctor insisted.

Ro shook his head sadly. "I have no money for the hospital."

"Well, you had better find it somewhere before that thing ruptures," the doctor said sternly.

Ro walked out of the office, his lips moving in earnest prayer. "Lord, I know no way to get that much money. If I really must have this operation, then you'll have to provide the funds."

CHAPTER 6

A Crucial Decision

Ro had been helping with publicity for the upcoming
YFC rally that would feature Bob Pierce. Now he had to
tell Cyril Thompson that he could not hang any more
poster signs. His stomach ached so badly that he could
not pedal his rented bicycle a single block.

To his surprise, Ro found the big, affable Pierce at the
Thompsons' breakfast table. Ro stood silently while Cyril
Thompson made the introductions, not wanting to inter-
rupt the visitor's meal. But Pierce was eager to talk.

"I was so impressed with your message in Calcutta,"
Ro said sincerely. "We met briefly afterward. You may
not remember."

Pierce smiled as if he did. He had met many people
in his Asian travels, but now he took time to get to know
Ro. He asked about his tribe, his schoolwork, his translation, and his future plans. Ro was so enthralled by the
genuine loving spirit of Pierce that he forgot his stomach-
ache. It seemed they had always been friends.

As well as coming to speak, Pierce was producing a
new missionary movie. He had come early to shoot some
footage. "Then I will not keep you," Ro said.

Pierce prayed with his tribal friend and then put his
arm around him and walked to the door to say good-bye.

"Buddy, I love you," he said, giving him a bear hug.
"God bless." Ro felt the American slipping something
into his pocket.

When he was alone, Ro looked and discovered 150
rupees. Enough for his operation! The next morning he
checked into the Kachwa Mission Hospital. The last fuzzy
words he heard before drifting under the anesthetic was
the missionary surgeon's prayer. "Lord, we dedicate our
hearts and hands to perform this surgery. . . ."

When he awoke, the doctor showed him a sharp stone
taken from his appendix. "Young man, it's a good thing
you came when you did. You'd never have lasted the
week."

Learning that Bob Pierce was still in India, he went to
express gratitude for the gift that had saved his life.
"How about going with me to Calcutta for a three-day
weekend rally?" Pierce suggested.

Ro was pleased to revisit the city and delighted at the
chance of getting to know this warm, loving American
better. Pierce was then setting up the Christian welfare
agency called World Vision to recruit American sponsors
for Korean war orphans.

During that weekend, Ro shared his longing to finish
the translation and to help his tribe spiritually and
materially.

"How would you like to go abroad for further education
that will help your translation work?" Pierce asked.

"Oh, I would love to." Ro sighed. This had been his
secret ambition since the days he had spent in line hoping
a GI would pick him for a land boy.

"Well, put in your application for a passport. It might
take a little time. I'll see if World Vision will sponsor you."

Ro filed for the passport, hoping it would be granted
by graduation time in the spring of 1954.

Early in 1954 he received a letter from the prime
minister's private secretary, inviting him to New Delhi.

He took along roommate Chiten Jamir, a young Ao Naga tribesman whom he had helped to become a Christian. Chiten also had ambitions to help his people and was eager to go.

Ro presented Nehru with some written information on tribal needs. One particular item on the list was a request for postal service for the Hmars. Ro had noted that the nearest post office to his home village of Phulpui was eighty miles away.

Nehru arranged for the students to meet with Kaka Kallelkar, the chairman of the Backward Classes Commission. After an hour-long discussion, he assured Ro that the next census and list of tribes would indeed include the Hmars. "Thank you, Mr. Chairman," Ro exclaimed happily, in appreciation for the great victory. "Now our Hmar young men will be eligible for scholarships."

While in New Delhi, Ro learned that all the important people in government read the *Amrita Bazar Patrika* and the *Leader* English-language newspapers. Articles on the Hmars in these publications would be an excellent way to make Indian leaders more aware of tribal needs. Back at Allahabad, he had hardly unpacked before he started to write.

As his senior year advanced, Ro polished the articles, studied for final exams, and translated more scripture. He also entered a twelve-page essay in a written debate the university's education department was conducting on the subject, "Should Religion Be Introduced in the University?" Basing his affirmative arguments mainly on scripture, he won first place.

"God has done so many wonderful things for me this year," he wrote his parents. "I don't know what he really wants me to be. Please pray with me that I will not miss his best."

Ro still hadn't heard from the passport office, but his

articles were accepted. Nehru read them and invited the
Hmar youth back, this time to stay at Constitution House,
the official national guest home.

Shortly after the end of his senior year, the young
tribesman with the infectious smile again visited the capital. When he entered the prime minister's office, Nehru
asked, "What can I do for you now?"

"Sir," Ro said directly, "suppose you had a son away in
school and every time you mailed him a letter you had to
walk eighty miles. How would you feel?"

"That would be a hard proposition," Nehru replied
with an enigmatic smile.

"Sir, since I was in high school, my father has walked
over six thousand miles to send me letters. I will be going
abroad for further study, and I would very much like a
post office near my home so my father will not have to
walk so far."

The prime minister was obviously impressed and began pumping Ro vigorously about the tribal lands, the
people, their languages, their problems. Ro sensed that
the powerful leader genuinely wished to identify with all
of India's disparate peoples.

As Ro was leaving, Nehru said, "Leave an address
where you may be reached. I will look into the postal
situation."

On his way back to the Hmar hills, Ro had an appointment to see Jairamdas Doulatram, who served as governor
over the adjoining states of Assam and Manipur. They
talked for an hour about tribal improvements. Governor
Doulatram pledged to arrange for a medical scholarship
for one of Ro's fellow tribesmen, and for scholarships for
Hmar girls, and said he would provide training for some
of the tribesmen in food preservation.

A train trip took Ro back to his native Manipur. While
he was in an Imphal hotel, chatting with two tribal friends,

a uniformed government messenger served him with an official-looking document. What have I done? Ro wondered as he looked at the paper. It requested his immediate attendance at a conference with the Postal Engineer and the Inspector of Post Offices.

Taking his friends along, Ro hurried over and was received with great deference. "Sir, Prime Minister Nehru's secretariat has instructed us to consult with you about opening four post offices for the Hmars," one official said. "Can you suggest some locations and postmasters?" While his friends stood agape, Ro picked out four sites for the first post offices in the tribe and gave four names, none of whom were relatives.

Upon reaching Phulpui, he found that news of his reception by the prime minister and the governor and of the plans for the new post offices had preceded him. He had become a celebrity. Chawnga and Daii beamed. "We must praise the Lord for the opportunities he has sent you," his father said.

Ro's accomplishments quickly spread across Hmar land, and one day a delegation came to ask that he help organize a Hmar political party. "We have no hospitals, no roads, no schools of our own. You met the prime minister and won post offices for us. You can help us in these ways also." The group stayed two days until Ro consented to serve as the organizing chairman of the new party.

Ro was excited and a little awed by the responsibility thrust upon him. He discussed the situation with Chawnga.

"Why, my father, they might even elect me as the leader of the new party. What do you think of my being in politics?"

"It is a very dangerous thing to be a politician, my son," Chawnga said slowly. "In our tribe or any tribe."

"Dangerous? In what way is it dangerous?"

"People's memories are very brief. They will praise you today and curse you tomorrow."

"But I could help our people in so many ways. I know English, I have met the prime minister, and I have finished my B.A. I am the most qualified to lead our tribe from obscurity."

"Perhaps it would be all right to help get the party established. But I feel God has higher plans for you than as a politician. While you go to the convention, your mother and I will remain here and pray for you."

Ro arranged for the convention to be held in July in the centrally located village of Parbung. Parbung, the second-largest town in the Hmar area, was known for its frank-speaking, politically oriented people. News of what was happening in Parbung would quickly travel to all the tribe.

He wrote letters to Prime Minister Nehru, Indira Gandhi, Governor Doulatram, and many others, informing them of the plans. He sent messages by runners to key tribesmen in every clan. He hoped for full participation and representation of all the tribe.

News of the upcoming convention inevitably reached the Mizo Union, which had been planting seeds of rebellion in tribes throughout northeast India. The Mizos did all they could to frustrate Ro's plans, even spreading false information that the convention had been called off. But they were unsuccessful, and on the appointed day some two hundred Hmar delegates from the various clans met in the school building in Parbung.

The first order of business Ro presented to the convention was a name for their new political party. "I would like to suggest Hmar National Congress. The word 'congress' will keep us in touch with the leading political party of India, and the use of the name Hmar will help bring our tribe into national prominence."

They agreed unanimously to this. Then they adopted a platform that would give Hmars an effective role in the political planning of the district. They wanted to be identified with India and have representation in national affairs. Plans were made to increase the gross income of the people and bring new roads and educational facilities. A feeling of excitement prevailed as they concluded their first day's business. Tomorrow they would elect a leader.

Ro was exhilarated as he walked along the ridge on which Parbung was built, toward the home he was staying in on the north side of town. What if they chose me? he asked the starry night. Then I would not only be well known in my tribe but in all India. I would get my name in the papers. I would return to New Delhi to consult with the leaders of our nation. Why, I might even become a Member of Parliament!

After a night of much dreaming but little sleeping, Ro returned to the school auditorium. There four groups were chosen to nominate candidates for the office of president. When the groups returned, Ro was asked to go to a classroom where he would not be able to see the election proceedings.

I've been nominated, he realized when he was asked to leave. Too bad I was asked to leave first; now I don't know who my competitors are.

"Lord, help me to be humble and to seek your will in this matter. You know how many plans I have for my people and how very much I want to help them. But make me willing to serve my people even if they don't choose me to be their leader."

The sound of much applause reached his ears, and he knew the convention had made its choice. Someone called him back into the room. As he stepped back on the platform to resume his duties as chairman, the vice-moderator told him quietly, "You have been unanimously elected.

There were no other nominees. We will give you a few minutes to collect your thoughts before you address the convention."

Ro sat heavily into his seat on the platform. Unanimously elected. What an honor! he thought as tears stung his eyes. What a responsibility! He looked out at the sea of expectant faces. "Lord, make me worthy of their confidence."

When he stood to address them, the entire audience came to its feet simultaneously. All chatter ceased, as they paid him homage by greeting him with absolute pin-drop silence. He swallowed hard, so his voice would not quiver as he told them, "I accept the responsibility to lead the tribe for the next four years. I thank you for your display of confidence."

His emotions were welling up, and he realized he was fighting a losing battle as he tried to control his voice. "My—my acceptance speech will have to wait," he told them. "I will write out something and address you tomorrow night. But I pledge to you now to use any knowledge that I have acquired these past few years for the good of the tribe. The Hmars *will* be brought to a prominent place in Indian society!"

As the delegates left the meeting place, the news was spread. Soon signals were being beamed by flashlight from one village to the next until the entire Hmar tribal nation had received the message: THE HMARS HAVE A NEW LEADER. ROCHUNGA SON OF CHAWNGA!

The next day, as Ro marched proudly over to the meeting place, the sun shone brilliantly and a light breeze was blowing. Small children scampered around him, cheering. Curious women peered at him through their windows. He felt like a king, and all the world seemed to be smiling at him.

As he entered the assembly he was greeted with a standing ovation and a round of applause. The business of the day seemed routine. They discussed plans, fees, membership requirements, division of the area into districts, a national headquarters. Everything seemed to be building toward the meeting to be held that evening.

As they broke for the evening meal, a runner brought Ro some mail. He quickly selected three important-looking envelopes to open. Indira Gandhi and the Governor of Assam both sent congratulations and good wishes. The third letter was from Allahabad, reporting that he had successfully passed his University examination.

At the bottom of the pile was a copy of an overseas cable sent from Toronto, Canada. It was a message from Watkin Roberts, and it read: INFORM ROCHUNGA PUDAITE MY FRIENDS AND I WILL PAY FOR INTENSIVE BIBLE TRAINING IN GLASGOW OR LONDON STOP CABLE DECISION.

Ro was stunned. He had had no idea that Mr. Young Man even knew he existed. Since he hadn't heard from the passport application, he had assumed it was not the Lord's will that he study abroad. Now, just when he was on the verge of accepting the political leadership of his people, this door had opened.

As he stood staring at the cable, he was called to the feast. "New president," his host asked, "what's wrong? Eat and be merry. You are destined to lead us into greatness and fame."

Troubled by the decision that faced him, he went to the feast and read the letters from Indira Gandhi and Governor Doulatram. Then he asked to postpone the acceptance speech until the next day.

Rising the next morning while darkness still lingered, he walked out to an old *jhum* house in a deserted field. For an hour he prayed there, pouring his feelings out to God.

"Lord God," he cried, "if you hear me, tell me what to do. If I reject the presidency, the new party I have brought into being may die. My people may lose hope. If I take it and remain here, I may never be able to finish the Bible translation. Tell me what to do," he implored. "I am willing to follow either path."

In a moment the words *Glasgow, Glasgow, Glasgow* began ringing in his heart. Fully assured that this was a direct answer to his prayer, he returned to face the expected displeasure of his people.

Who will lead them? he wondered. If there were someone well qualified to take my place, the decision would not be so difficult. I must believe that the Lord knows what is best for our tribe. Surely this will work out to their benefit in the long run.

He returned to his quarters to find his friends still sleeping. He washed his face, drank a cup of tea, and then prepared a new speech to deliver before the installation that evening. He felt he was turning his back on his opportunity for great power and fame, but he had to follow God's leadership. Could he make them understand this?

If anyone noticed how subdued and serious he seemed that day, no one mentioned it. The hours dragged on. It was hard to be enthusiastic about plans he would have no part in implementing.

When he came to the platform that evening, some of the tribal leaders came up with a distinguished *puondum* cloth, traditionally bestowed on tribesmen who brought honor to the tribe by their accomplishments. The taking of the head of an enemy or the killing of a hundred wild animals to feed the tribe was considered necessary to merit a *puondum* cloth.

The leaders draped the red cloth with its black and white striped design upon Ro's shoulders. "Now that you have finished your B.A. and distinguished yourself educationally, we bestow this cloth," said the spokesman. "You have brought honor to all Hmars, and we have confidence that you will lead our tribe to greatness."

Ro's heart was pounding furiously as they brought forth next the feathered headdress given in past times to great Hmar chiefs. The long *vakul* feathers of the "king bird" were placed on his head. "Oh, Lord, how can I turn my back on this mandate from my people? Are you sure you want me to leave?" Again the words *Glasgow, Glasgow* rang in his ears.

He stepped forward to the podium and looked into the faces smiling up at him: such an eager audience, so expectant. "Lord help me," he breathed as he began.

"Something I had never anticipated has happened," he told them. "I had no thought that anything could intervene. But a cable came very unexpectedly." He explained as best he could that he felt God was leading him to continue his education abroad. The crowd held its breath.

"I therefore tender my resignation. I want all of us here to pray about another man to take my place. I'll do all I can to help."

For a moment the audience sat in stunned silence. Then, as the shock wore off, there was a rustle in the crowd.

"No."

"It can't be!"

"We have no one else to lead us."

The noise grew as the reaction spread through the delegates. Some of the more spiritual agreed that Ro should follow the Lord's leadership, but a few disgruntled men said, "He is leaving us because a better opportunity has come."

The choice was finally made to elect Lungawi, Ro's cousin, to replace him. Lungawi was a college student and spoke English. He had not traveled as extensively as Ro and had not had the opportunity of meeting important people, but the delegates were determined to be unanimously behind their leader.

Ro's spirit was uneasy. He had so many plans, but he had no confidence that they would be carried out without his leadership. "I'll pray for you," he told his cousin sincerely. "If there is any way I can help, I'll be glad to do so."

The only Hmars who had ever traveled outside the country had gone as soldiers. Ro was the first to go as a civilian. Chawnga and two friends accompanied him on the long hike to Silchar and waited until he boarded his bus to the airport. From the window Ro snapped their picture with his prized Agfa camera.

Stopping in Calcutta, Ro preached at the church he had attended as a student. Afterward the members gave him a bon voyage party and Pastor Walter Corlett pronounced, "On behalf of the William Carey Baptist Church, I commission you, Rochunga Pudaite, as our Indian missionary to the west!"

Looking at the smiling faces brought back the memory of those who loved him back home, in the tribe. Ro was leaving so many friends, so many who had confidence in him. What kind of people will I meet in far-off England, he wondered.

CHAPTER 7

Mr. Young Man!

"Will you be having a cocktail before dinner, sir? Or just a soft drink?"

"Would you like a pillow and a blanket?"

"How about a magazine? Do you have a preference?"

The glamorous Dutch stewardesses on KLM's Super Constellation flight to London made Ro feel like a king. All his life he had associated white faces with power and authority. Now to have three beautiful girls dressed like fashion models to wait on him was a delightful new experience.

Too excited for sleep, he took out his Bible and read from Isaiah 43:

> Fear not: for I have redeemed thee; *I have called thee by thy name; thou art mine.* When thou passest through the waters, I will be with thee, and through the rivers, they shall not overflow thee: when thou walkest through the fire, thou shall not be burned; neither shall the flame kindle upon thee. For I am the Lord thy God.

What reassurance! Surely if the Lord had called him by

name and claimed him as his own, he would receive
guidance. The waters of testings would not be too deep
nor the fires of afflictions too warm. Through all, the Lord
would see him through.

The Bible Training Institute had only a hundred or so
students. Only one other besides Ro was a college graduate. Some of his classmates hadn't even finished high
school. While Ro didn't want to make them feel inferior,
he did want to make the most of his time abroad.

Fortunately, Principal McBeth understood the problem
and arranged for the young foreigner to take special classes
in Hebrew and Greek at Glasgow University.

In the spring, Ro began receiving invitations to speak.
He usually traveled by bus, the cheapest transportation,
since the churches and assemblies expected him to pay his
fare from the stipend. (The Scots lived up to their reputation for thrift by giving honorariums of about ten shil-
lings—$1.35 for a Sunday.)

Whenever he could, Ro visited his friends the Nielsons,
a family that had befriended him shortly after he arrived
at the Institute. One morning he awoke at their home and
looked out the window at a white world. Thinking he
was dreaming, he lay back down and tried to sleep some
more, but no, he was awake. and the world was white!

He went to the bathroom, splashed cold water on his
face, and then turned slowly back to the window. That
same strange white stuff still shrouded the ground. He ran
downstairs in his bathrobe and asked Mrs. Nielson, "Am
I awake or asleep?"

"You are wide awake," was the reassuring response.

"Then why has the ground turned white?"

"Oh, that's just snow. A bit early this year."

Ro dashed out the back door and scooped up a heaping
handful. "Praise the Lord! Hallelujah!" he sang out in
delighted ecstasy. "My sins are washed away, and I'm as

clean and white as this snow." He brought a bucketful into the house and sat gazing at it until it melted away.

Chapter by chapter, Ro's translation manuscript kept piling up. He made frequent trips to London to consult with Dr. William Bradnock of the British and Foreign Bible Society, who had agreed to publish the Hmar Bible, and was sometimes a guest in his Kent country home.

Once on the train going to Kent he settled himself near a window. A dignified, buxom English lady in a fur coat swished into the compartment and sat next to him.

"Excuse me," she said. "What nationality are you?"

"I am Indian, from India," Ro replied politely.

Her face clouded into a frown. "You fellows from poor countries!" She bristled contemptuously. "You come and enjoy our benefits of education and health, and my husband has to pay the taxes!"

Ro thought she must be joking. He had never encountered such prejudice before. "If I were not here, madam, would your husband stop paying taxes?" he asked sincerely.

The question sparked a fury of verbal abuse that went on and on until her breath was spent.

"I—I'm sorry, madam," Ro stammered. "I didn't mean to insult you." But she was not to be placated. Gathering a second wind, she continued the tirade for a half hour until they reached her station.

As she started to get out, Ro jumped ahead of her and took her two suitcases and carried them out of the train. As he set them on the pavement, he looked her in the eye and said softly, "Here is your luggage, madam. It was most enlightening to be with you. I am sorry for the many hardships we have caused you and countless others in England. Please accept my apology and thank you for sharing with me from your heart. Thank you."

He bowed deeply and jumped back on the train. Wav-

ing his hand, he called to her, "Good-bye, and God bless
you." She stared after him, open-mouthed. As the train
began chugging out of the station a smile softened her
face, and she waved a handkerchief and called "Good-
bye," too.

He was more shocked on another trip when he walked
along the shore of a lake. Rounding a line of bushes, he
heard giggling and looked to see a group of naked young
men and women rolling in blankets in plain view. Never
would Hmars appear so brazenly immodest. The sight so
startled him that he took off running, never looking
back.

Back in Glasgow at the turn of the year, the Christians
were preparing for Billy Graham's upcoming crusade. Professor D. P. Thompson, the Director of Evangelism for
the Church of Scotland, invited Ro to travel with him
under the Tell Scotland Campaign, the group that had invited Dr. Graham to their country. During these weekend trips Ro had the joy of helping several people come
to know his Lord.

One day while Ro was having lunch in the Bible Training Institute's dining hall, the Institute secretary came
running breathlessly to announce a telephone call from
Billy Graham. It was actually Dr. Graham's personal assistant, Dr. Paul Maddox, asking if Ro could come to the
Northern British Hotel for a chat with the evangelist.

"I'll be there in five minutes," Ro exclaimed. Forgetting
his half-finished meal, he dashed the ten city blocks to
the hotel in record time.

He was panting when he entered the lounge where Dr.
Maddox was waiting. The two went up to the Grahams'
room. Dr. Graham and his wife, Ruth, were sitting on the
bed, and George Beverly Shea and Cliff Barrows were on
a trunk. They all greeted Ro. Then the evangelist waved
him to the couch.

"I've heard reports from various prayer groups that your whole tribe back in India is praying for our campaign in Scotland," Graham said.

"This is true," Ro replied, amazed at how at ease he felt with the friendly Americans. "My father has organized all-night prayer meetings, a chain of prayer from one village to another."

"And is it also true that your father walked over a hundred miles to read a Bible after he was converted?" the evangelist asked.

"Yes," said Ro, smiling. "Missionaries were not allowed in Hmar territory, so my father walked to a neighboring state to get Bible training. Then he returned to evangelize his own people."

"A remarkable story," the team agreed, and they continued asking questions about this indigenous work in India.

"And now I am translating the Word into Hmar so that my people can read the Bible in their own language," Ro explained.

"I wish I could stay and talk with you longer," Graham said, "but I have a luncheon appointment. You will forgive me if I leave. Stay and talk with the others."

As Graham shook Ro's small hand with his huge one he asked, "Where are you studying?"

"At the Bible Training Institute," Ro replied.

"Are you satisfied?"

"No."

"If you would like to attend Wheaton College, I could arrange it," he offered.

"Well, I've already been offered scholarships at Oxford, the University of Glasgow, and the College at Edinburgh, but I'll pray about it."

"Fine. Let me know what you decide," Graham said, and left.

Ro stayed another half hour and visited with Ruth Graham and the musical members of the team. He was so impressed at meeting such famous people. He remembered how he had wondered when leaving India as to what kind of people he would meet in England. He had never expected anything like this.

Wheaton was the school he had planned to attend when Bob Pierce had offered to help him through school in America. When he did not hear from his first passport application he had given up the idea, but now maybe, just maybe, the Lord was going to lead that way after all.

While letters moved back and forth to the States concerning his admission to Wheaton, Ro finished the first draft of the Hmar New Testament. With a strong sense of accomplishment he showed the manuscript to Dr. Bradnock, who patiently described the next step of revision and correction.

Upon receiving the good news of his acceptance by Wheaton, Ro applied for his U.S. visa. The consul in Glasgow insisted on seeing a birth certificate. Ro told him that when he was born such documents were not being issued in tribal areas of India. "You can see that I have indeed been born, and I'm obviously not of British descent," he argued gently. But only after considerable persuasion was the visa granted.

World Vision had sent $150 for transportation, not enough to fly but perhaps enough for an inexpensive steamship passage. Ro was booked on a ship sailing from Southampton to Montreal. There was just the right amount of time to go to Chadwick, England, where he had agreed to act as a native informant for the Wycliffe Bible Translators training school.

On the fifth day the ship slipped into the St. Lawrence Seaway. Ro walked grandly around the deck to see Canada from both sides. The majestic cliffs, the carpet of green forest above them, and the sun yellowing the mountaintops made him feel he was entering a promised land.

At Montreal he boarded the train that would take him

on the next lap of his journey. As he listened to the soothing *clickety-clack* of the wheels that were bringing him closer to Toronto he thought of the friend who would be waiting for him. Watkin Roberts—Pu Tlangval, Mr. Young Man, as the tribespeople still called him—was to meet him at the station.

Ro's seatmate wanted to talk about uranium and its possibilities for the future in India, but Ro found it difficult to concentrate. He wanted to be polite and keep up his end of the conversation, but all he could think was, I am going to meet Watkin Roberts. I am going to meet Watkin Roberts. I am really going to meet Mr. Young Man!

He had heard about him all his life. He had seen his picture and even corresponded with him during the past year. But to actually meet him in person was a privilege he had never expected to have. Next to his own father, there was no man he held in higher esteem than the spiritual father of his tribe.

Will he like me? he wondered. Is he the type of person that you must impress at your first meeting? I hope not, for I shall surely feel shy and humble in his presence. And his wife. What is she like? Does she share his love for tribal people? My, this trip seems long. I had no idea it was so far from Montreal to Toronto. I hope we don't arrive late; I wouldn't want to keep them waiting.

The closer he got to his destination, the more excited Ro became. Ottawa . . . Belleville . . . Oshawa. They would be there soon. He sat on the edge of his seat, staring out the window for the last hundred miles.

At last the conductor came down the aisle. "Toronto. Next stop is Toronto."

Before the train jolted to a final stop in the terminal, Ro was standing on the steps peering into the crowd. As he stepped down, an aging, white-haired man with sparkling eyes limped toward him. "*I dam a lawm maw,*" he called to Ro in beautiful flowing Lushai. "You are really well, aren't you! My, my! Think of Chawnga's son being in Toronto. I like your name. Rochunga: God's Highest Treasure! So good, so very good to have you here."

A broad smile burst across Ro's face. The warmth and sincerity of the greeting made him forget to be shy. Why, it seemed he and Mr. Young Man had been friends always.

Watkin Roberts introduced his wife, Gladys, and daughter, Ruth, and they started toward the car. "I still love the people of India, Rochunga. I've never stopped praying for them, and for your tribe especially. And now you've come to America to complete your education. What an answer to prayer!

"How is your father?" Roberts asked as they drove through the streets of Toronto. "Does he still preach with the same fervor?"

"My father is well," Ro replied. "And he preaches just the same. Wherever he travels the people crowd around him."

"He can spellbind any audience," the old man reminisced. "Many times I have thought how tremendous it would be to bring him to America. But he doesn't speak English, and that would require a good interpreter."

As they turned the corner at a busy intersection Roberts seemed hardly conscious of the traffic around them. "And how is my old friend Pastor Taisena?"

"Pastor Taisena was expelled from Manipur during the days of political persecution. But after independence he returned and is serving the Lord there now."

As they settled themselves in the Robertses comfortable home, the questioning continued. "And Lalchanliana. How is he?"

"Lalchanliana is a very fine man, but he smokes too much," Ro replied.

Roberts laughed at the frank appraisal. "Yes," he agreed, "all your mountain people smoke too much. It hurt me to see such young children start puffing on the traditional pipes, but I never condemned the practice. I certainly am glad to see that you don't smoke. How did you come to quit?"

"Well, I was a heavy smoker until I was in college in Calcutta. I had very little money, and I was convicted about sending the Lord's money up in smoke. But I couldn't stop.

"Then one day I heard an appeal for Tibetan Bibles. I was so touched I gave every cent I had, even my carfare. As I was walking home I passed a tobacco shop, and the aroma called to me. I went up to my room and got out the few cigarettes I had left and I destroyed them. Then I took up my Bible and prayed, 'Lord, let these hands that hold your Word never again touch tobacco.' And I never have."

"I like that," Roberts said heartily, nodding his large head in agreement. "God blesses young men with such character. I like your way."

Then Ro had an opportunity to ask a question himself. "Pu Tlangval, how did you come to send that cable at such an auspicious time?"

"Oh, for quite a number of years I've been praying for someone from the Hmars to come to the West for special training. I've felt for some time that the day of foreign missions in India is coming to a close. I saw that if we were to continue the Indo-Burma Pioneer Mission and enlarge its ministry, a tribesman must be prepared to assume leadership.

"One morning after I had finished praying I heard over the radio that an Indian lady was to speak at the Toronto Youth for Christ rally. I invited her to my office. It was Winnie Bonar, who told me about you. I found that you are the son of Chawnga, my wonderful friend and fellow soldier.

"I bowed to pray—I cannot kneel because polio has

crippled my leg—and I sensed the Lord saying, *Send him a cable now; send him a cable now.* So I sent the message. That's all."

Ro leaned forward, his dark features intense. "It must truly have been of the Lord, Pu Tlangval. On the very day it arrived I was . . ." And the two friends talked on late into the night about the Lord's working in Ro's life.

As he left for Wheaton three days later, Ro was over-whelmed with a sense of gratitude for having had the opportunity to meet this dignified, determined old man who had meant so much to his tribe. He left with a re-newed confidence that, as his father had assured him long before, God's love had preceded him unto this new horizon.

CHAPTER 8

Dating and Waiting

On the commuter train from Chicago's Loop to suburban Wheaton, Ro marveled at the sights flashing by his window. Did everybody in Chicago live in a palatial home and drive a car? And the crowds getting on and off at stations: so many people, and he didn't know even one. As best as he could figure, there were only six people in the United States he had ever met—all missionaries—and none lived nearby.

As he stood in one line after another matriculating at Wheaton College, the tribesman listened to students laughing and calling to friends they had not seen since the start of summer vacation. These vociferous Americans certainly seemed friendly. Like Britishers, they were tall and pale, but they had very different accents.

It was late afternoon when he moved into the last line. His stomach was growling, for he had not eaten all day. When he reached the desk, the lady informed him that graduate students were not permitted to live in a school dorm.

"But for a foreigner it would be such a good opportunity to meet some of my fellow students," he protested.

"I'm sorry, Mr. Pudaite," she said kindly. "School policy. You'll have to find a room off campus."

Ro walked along a tree-lined residential street, knocking on doors. "No, our extra room has been taken. . . .

No. . . . No. . . . No." Then, at 103 North Main Street, a large smiling blond woman showed him a cheerful room in her home. "Oh, this will be wonderful, Mrs. Bartlett," he said. "I'll take it."

The evening shadows were growing long when Ro walked into a corner grocery to buy something to eat. He shuffled up and down the crowded aisles peering at the strange labels. He wasn't used to the precooked items and had never tried cold cuts. Finally he selected a can of peaches and a fruit drink and returned to his lonely room for his first meal in the United States.

When the leaves on the oaks and elms that shaded Wheaton's tree-lined streets began their fall fashion show, Ro was immersed in work. Besides his classwork, he worked three hours each evening in the school library, toiled at revising the Hmar New Testament, and as inspiration came did a devotional book for Hmars titled *This Mountain Spring*. With church services on Sunday, he had only Saturday for free time.

"You're too much of a grind," Howard Wood, a roommate at Mrs. Bartlett's, announced one day. "All you do is work and study and translate. What you need is a date. How about letting me fix you up with a girl for this weekend?"

"A date!" Ro gulped, even though he was now twenty-eight years old. "I've never had a date. I wouldn't know how to act! Certainly not on an American-style date."

"We'll make it a double date, and I'll give you lessons. It's easy."

Reluctantly, Ro agreed.

On the eventful evening Ro marched up to Janet's door and knocked. A cold sweat gripped him.

"Good evening, Rochunga," she said politely.

He bowed ceremoniously and replied, "Good evening."

I just knew it, he thought. She's tall, really tall. Why, she must be six feet. And Howard didn't tell me that

Tennesseans sound so strange. How will I ever understand her?

"Well," said Janet pleasantly, trying to put Ro at ease, "you're right on the dot!"

Ro looked down at his feet. Then he shuffled them in bewilderment. He didn't see any dot.

In his confusion he forgot Howard's instructions about taking her elbow to help her down the steps. He just scurried along after her, trying to keep up with her long-legged strides. When he did reach for her elbow, he realized she was too tall for him to guide gracefully, so he walked on tiptoes all the way to the car.

Everything seemed to go wrong. His coat caught in the door, and he thought she was pulling on him. When they got to the restaurant, he watched as Howard smoothly pushed in the chair for his date, so he tried it too. But Janet was already seated and the chair wouldn't budge. With a sense of rising panic Ro bent down, put his shoulder to the back of the chair, and shoved. It was like pushing a boulder!

After dinner, Howard asked what kind of ice cream they wanted.

Ro didn't know what to order, so he said, "I'll take a cone." The others ordered sundaes, which were served in dainty dishes poised on doily-topped plates. Ro felt like a foolish child licking on his cone.

Most of the conversation was beyond him. He didn't know who or what they were talking about, and Janet's accent just compounded the problem. To the Asian's great relief, Howard dropped him off first and then went to take the girls home.

It took several days for the trauma in cultural shock to wear off. By then Ro had resolved never to date again unless it was absolutely necessary. Surely the Lord could find him a life's partner without the embarrassment of dating.

Ro's finances were little better than his social life. School fees were being paid by World Vision. The student library job covered incidental expenses. Then he received word that a medical student he had helped get a scholarship from the Governor of Assam was having trouble making ends meet. Ro immediately began sending him a regular portion from the small salary paid for the library work.

The cold Illinois winter blew in with an icy blast. The temperature plummeted. He had survived a winter in Scotland without a topcoat, but he realized he'd never make it in Illinois. The trips to and from the campus got colder and colder. One day as he shivered in the classroom, a student told him that clothing could be bought cheaply at a rummage sale being held at a local Catholic church.

Ro didn't know what rummage meant, but he went along hopefully. Looking through some topcoats, he struck up a conversation with a friendly nun. He told her of his experience with Christ, and she said she had met Christ only a few months earlier herself. He beamed in delight as the sister related her conversion experience.

As they talked, a tan coat from the pile caught his fancy. When he tried it on, it seemed hand-tailored for his narrow shoulders. But the price tag said $35.

"Is there some arrangement I could make to get this coat?" he asked the nun. "I need it very much, but I can't afford the full price."

"How much money do you have with you?" she asked.

He emptied his pockets and came up with $1.50.

"Take the coat." She smiled. "God loves you, and I love you too. I will pray that your time in America will be most profitable."

Ro floated home feeling indeed a Child of the King. The Lord had provided him with a new coat that was not only warm and comfortable but flattering, too. And he had found a new friend and sister in the Lord.

One morning early in December, Mrs. Bartlett asked her foreign boarder to come home right after his last class. "Don't go to the library, don't eat in the Student Union, just come straight home, please," she insisted.

Ro thought this rather unusual, but having become close to the kind-hearted widow whom he regarded as his American mother, he promised to do so.

That afternoon he walked in and there were all his friends from church and school. "Surprise! Surprise! Happy birthday, Ro!" they shouted, and they began singing.

Nobody had ever sung "Happy Birthday" to the young Asian before, for the Hmars do not celebrate birthdays. He could not stop the tears from spilling over, he was so touched. There was a beautiful cake, and everyone brought envelopes. After they had eaten the cake, he began opening them. In all he received $127, enough to meet his personal expenses for the whole winter. His heart overflowed with joy at the love expressed by these new friends. "I'll remember this day as long as I live," he told them.

One day Ro was introduced to Eunice Finstrom, the daughter of a retired missionary to India. When she mentioned her father's longing for a good Indian dinner, Ro invited them to Mrs. Bartlett's house for "an authentic native meal."

The old missionary ate with great gusto, fondly remembering his days on the Asian subcontinent. He enjoyed himself so much that Ro was glad he had invited them.

"Do you have a car, Rochunga?" Ben Finstrom asked as they were leaving. When Ro shook his head, the old man chuckled. "Well, I have one that was given to me, an old thirty-nine Buick. My eyes are too poor for me to drive any longer, so it just sits in the street. If you'll come and pick it up, you may have it."

A car! Ro hadn't even dared to dream of having his very

own transportation. He was so excited he could hardly wait to see it.

Howard went with him to get the old jalopy. It was filthy from sitting for years in the Chicago weather, but Ro thought it was beautiful. They got it back to Wheaton, and Ro washed and scrubbed and polished the old relic until it positively shone. "Terrific!" He sighed.

After Howard explained the mechanics of the machine, Ro carefully drove up and down and around the block until he felt confident of himself. Then he applied for a license and passed the test.

Another pleasant surprise came when Watkin Roberts journeyed from Toronto "just to see you, Rochunga." The old man was already seventy, and his foot seemed to drag much worse than the year before. But his mind was sharp and his heart warm.

By this time Ro had set up an improvised office in Mrs. Bartlett's basement. Mr. Young Man seemed pleased when he saw the piles of books and manuscripts spread across the desk where Ro had been busy revising the translation. Slowly letting himself drop into a chair, the old man's eyes sparkled with purity and purpose.

"I'm getting old," he declared. "These legs do not obey orders any more," and he hit his polioed leg lightly with his walking stick. "For nearly thirty years I have been praying for someone from the Hmars to carry on the work God began with me among your people.

"I believe the national movement we started should be carried on with national leadership. I've come here to see if God might have said something to you."

It was hard to resist the plea, but Ro realized he was being asked to head an organization that was no organization at all! It had no assets, no capital, no board, no officials, not even a mailing list. All the Indo-Burma Pioneer Mission had was a group of native workers who loved the Lord and wished to serve him, and an old man on the other side of the world who wrote encouraging letters.

"Pu Tlangval, I cannot say yes now. I have my studies to complete. I *must* finish the Hmar New Testament. It is a commitment I must fulfill."

The light in the septuagenarian's eyes began to dim like the turning down of a hurricane lamp. His shoulders drooped and his head bowed. He cleared his throat and then slowly lifted his head. "Rochunga, you know how much I love India, your people for whom I have given my life. I was not permitted to live with them at Senvon, but in my heart I have been dwelling with them for nearly fifty years."

"I'll pray about it," Ro promised. "Next week I'm going to Washington, D.C. World Vision is paying my fare. Dr. Pierce wants me to see the capital of this great nation. Then in August I will come to you with my decision."

The old man seemed content with that. "My prayers will follow you, Rochunga. I will ask God to make the way plain."

In Toronto a few weeks later, Ro reported to Watkin Roberts. He had considered his answer carefully and prayerfully, for he did not want to hurt the beloved Mr. Young Man.

"As I finish the translation work, I will be speaking in churches. I will tell those wishing to help India to send the money to you. We can be building up a mailing list—"

"But I want you to take over and build the mission," Watkin Roberts interrupted.

"I am continuing to ask the Lord's guidance. If he so leads, perhaps I can become the Organizing Secretary in a year or two."

"Yes, yes," the old man murmured. "I can wait. But can the lost multitudes of India?"

CHAPTER 9

God's Chosen One

An interesting letter came from Ro's cousin Luoia. "I am now chief of Sielmat village." he wrote. "Would you like twenty acres of land for missionary work?"

This was exciting. Sielmat was one of the fastest growing Hmar towns in northeast India and was connected with the state capital by a good road. It was only thirty-five miles from the Imphal airport, which had a daily flight to Calcutta, and would be a much better location for a headquarters than either Senvon or Phulpui.

Twenty acres was enough for a boarding school, a hospital, even a college!

Ro accepted the generous offer by return mail. Then he wrote his father and Mr. Thanglung, asking if they would move to this location.

Next he inveigled special permission from the Indian government for Watkin Roberts to visit the "restricted" northeast tribal area. Persuading Mr. Young Man that he should go personally and investigate the Sielmat site was no problem. For almost thirty years the ex-missionary had longed to see his beloved tribal friends. Even a crippled leg, mounting blood pressure, and an ulcer couldn't keep him away.

From village to village, Hmar messengers carried the

glad news: "Mr. Young Man is returning." There was wild excitement throughout Hmar land, for by this time 80 percent of the tribe had become Christians.

A cheer rang up from the delegation on hand to greet him when he limped from the aircraft at Imphal. The ladies insisted he allow them to carry him on a ceremonial mat to the waiting jeep which would take him to Sielmat.

There a pig was already roasting in his honor. When they gathered for the feast, a committee presented him with the special *puondum* cloth reserved for paying homage to great men. He was the first white man ever to be so honored. But his greatest thrill came upon seeing the multitude of tribesmen bow in thanksgiving to God before the feast began. These transformed lives were his real "crown."

He would have liked to revisit Senvon, where he had answered the invitation of Chief Kamkholun forty-seven years before, but the hundred-mile hike was not possible. Instead he had to be content with villages that could be reached by jeep.

Traveling with Chawnga, Mr. Thanglung, and other Hmar church leaders, he kept hearing English words that had crept into the Hmar language: *Bible school. Conference. Newspaper. Committee. Pastor. Bible woman.* He was certain most of the Hmars didn't even realize the origin of such words, but they had become part of their vocabulary largely through the influence of the gospel.

At Lakhipur he attended the annual assembly of the church that represented the majority of Hmar Christians. He approved as the leaders voted to merge the church administration with the new development planned at Sielmat. It pleased him immensely to know that mission and church would be one entity.

Before ending his nostalgic journey, Mr. Young Man asked the Hmar church leaders what they thought of Ro becoming the mission's Organizing Secretary in the United States. They were thrilled. "We've always felt there was capable leadership within our tribe."

Roberts returned and reported this statement. "They have full confidence in you, Rochunga. You must not disappoint them."

"You and my Hmar brothers honor me," Ro replied. "But I must finish my education and get the New Testament ready for publication. Then I will organize a board for raising funds here."

Ro was pushing hard on his Bible translation. He had hired a typist for $1 an hour while he worked in the library for $1.50.

By the spring of 1958 he felt the manuscript would soon be ready to take to London. With two of Mr. Thanglung's daughters studying nursing in England, he had another reason to make the trip. He had been exchanging letters with Hnemi, the elder, and hoped—just hoped—she might be the girl for him.

He wrote Mr. Thanglung of his plan to visit Hnemi and received a favorable reply. Then, two weeks before he planned to leave, Hnemi stopped writing. Busy with last-minute revisions, Ro thought little of it.

Upon arrival in London, he took the Hmar New Testament manuscript, revised and polished, to Dr. Bradnock. Then he drove a rented car to Reading, where the Thanglung girls were in training. The three were to spend a vacation in Southport with a friend of Ro's from Glasgow days.

Hnemi looked lovely to Ro. He could hardly wait to take her for a drive along the seashore. He double-pressed his shirt and donned a freshly cleaned suit. Surely, this is my hour, he thought. But there was no chemistry, no magic. She seemed ill at ease. They never got beyond small talk.

It must not be God's plan, he decided disappointedly. Perhaps I am to remain a bachelor all my days. He concluded that it would be best to act like a big brother to the sisters for the rest of the stay. He would just enjoy being with someone from home.

Ro felt a little sad at returning to Wheaton with no commitment for the future, but he felt assured that God was leading and knew he would make no mistakes. He would choose for him the best wife.

One afternoon he returned to Mrs. Bartlett's from classes and found the Hmar Student Association's magazine in his mail. It contained a list of young Hmars who had passed matriculation examinations and were going on to college. For the first time he noticed a girl's name. L. Rimawi was enrolled at St. Mary's College in Shillong, Assam.

Rimawi? Rimawi? Ah, she was one of the girls I taught English in 1953, he recalled. She must be the first girl from our tribe to go to college. I should write her congratulations.

Ro sent a small gift along with his note. A lovely thank-you letter came back, mentioning the English classes and telling how much the encouragement he gave then had meant to her.

Ro was prompted to write again. He wondered if she were having any problems as a Protestant attending a Roman Catholic college and asked if he could help in any way.

At the time he was feeling low, partly because of fatigue from long hours of study and energy-consuming efforts to raise funds for the mission work in India, partly because he had been away from home almost four years.

One Saturday morning he awoke restless and unhappy. Like the beginning of the murky monsoon weather in his homeland, the future seemed to stretch endlessly before him. Did I make a mistake in refusing the political leadership of my tribe? he wondered. Would I even now be in Parliament, mingling among the influential people of India, if I had not come west to study? Would I be helping my people more than I am now?

He slipped down to his tiny basement office to wrestle in prayer. Lunchtime came, and still he prayed. Finally he rose from his knees to get the mail, hoping for some encouragement.

There was a letter from Rimawi, written in English. She asked him to pray for her brother, Khuma, who was taking his B.A. final exams, and then went on, "You asked if I have problems. Yes, but I do not pray for an easy task and that all the barriers should be broken down for me. I only pray that God will give me the strength, in weakness his will to do, for he said, 'My grace is sufficient for thee.' "

Ro was so deeply touched by her resolute faith that he felt ashamed. Why should I feel discouraged? he asked himself. He went upstairs to his room, combed his hair, and went out for lunch. Rimawi's words walked with him, strangely warming his heart.

Later he read her letters over and over. He tried to frame her face in his memory but could only imagine luminous dark eyes smiling beneath smooth braids of black hair piled on her head. A search through his files revealed a picture he had taken that summer, but it was nearly five years old. She looked like a thousand other Hmar girls in their early teens. Certainly she had since matured. What did she look like now, at nineteen?

A letter came from Bob Pierce. "Would you join our World Vision team conducting summer pastors' conferences in Japan, Taiwan, Singapore, Burma, and India? All expenses will be paid."

India! He could make a side trip to his beloved hills. Home, family, friends, Rimawi—yes, definitely Rimawi. Praise the Lord.

With something really exciting to anticipate, Ro was his old self again—exuberant, enthusiastic, bubbling with optimism.

The galley proofs were coming now from the British and Foreign Bible Society. Checking and correcting them was a delight. To think—God's Word was at last being *printed* in Hmar!

In the spring of 1958 he completed the first board of directors of the Indo-Burma Pioneer Mission and was installed as president. In addition to Watkin Roberts, the founding members were: the Rev. John D. Jess, Dr. V. Raymond Edman, Dr. Clyde W. Taylor, Dr. Neil A. Winegarden, the Rev. James A. Watt, the Rev. Earl H. King, Douglas L. Mains, and Franklin A. Hinrichs.

Within the week Ro left to join the World Vision team for the pastors' conference in Japan. Fifteen hundred people came to pray, share fellowship and testimonies, participate in Bible study, and listen to inspiring teachers. Most of them could not have come without World Vision's financial assistance.

Ro spoke one night, thrilling them with his testimony, bringing tears to the eyes of the usually stoic Asians. Afterward, Bob Pierce pounded him on the back. "You were great, brother. You encouraged them. As an Asian you reach them in a way we Westerners can't."

The final conference was in Calcutta. From here Ro left for the hills of Manipur. What a welcome he received! There was feasting and rejoicing, with hundreds coming to Sielmat to hear him preach. There were cheers and exclamations and praise when he announced that the Hmar New Testament would soon be ready. Everywhere he went, young Hmars would come up and stare eyeball to eyeball and say, "Are you the one?" They meant, Are you the Rochunga Pudaite—the first from our tribe—who went to America?

One of his first acts as head of the mission was to call

a meeting of the Hmar Bible Translation Committee. During the discussion Mr. Thanglung stood up unexpectedly, tossed down some manuscript papers, and declared, "I am through. I resign from the committee." Questioning revealed that he was upset because all correspondence from the Bible Society had been channeled through Ro.

Ro invited his old friend to dinner to discuss the problem. There in the presence of his father, Chawnga, Ro promised Mr. Thanglung, "When the New Testament is printed, I will gladly turn the rest of the translation over to you and the committee. This will free me to raise financial support in the United States for the mission. We cannot educate our students and train pastors and evangelists with our own resources. The national government cannot help us. We must look to our American brethren."

Seeing that Ro really meant what he said, Mr. Thanglung relaxed and conceded that he had acted hastily. He would shepherd the Old Testament translation through.

Both Chawnga and Daii were anxious for a private talk with their "celebrity" son. There was so much coming and going that Chawnga had to ask in desperation that Ro set aside one evening for an "important" discussion with his parents. Ro agreed and assigned the cook to guard the door.

"Is everything well with you?" Ro asked politely. "Does Ramlien continue to watch over your welfare?"

They assured him that they were in good health and far from being dependent upon their older son, who was now a village pastor.

"My son, it is you we are concerned about," Daii said bluntly. "You are almost thirty-one years old and still unmarried. There are too many problems for a single man in the ministry, especially for one who is now the head of a mission."

"B-but I haven't found anyone yet," Ro stammered.

"But, my son," his mother persisted. "You have seen many girls since you came, have you not? Isn't there one that interests you? Even a little?"

"Mother," he said, feeling like a ten-year-old. "As head of the mission, with so many responsibilities, how can I go around looking over girls in the short time I have here? It is impossible!"

But Daii was determined. She surprised Ro with her next words. "Have you met a college girl named Rimawi? She is now studying in Shillong. She came here last year for the students' conference. We liked her very much."

"Oh, Mother!" Ro spoke with mock indignation. "Shillong is three hundred miles away! What would the church leaders think of my going so far to see a girl?"

But if God could work it out, I would truly like to meet her, he thought. If my parents approve of her, she must be very special.

What Ro hadn't told his parents was that he had already invited Rimawi to come to Sielmat during the Puja vacation in mid-October. Schools would be closed for two weeks during that Hindu festival, and he could see her then.

To his deep consternation a letter came from Rimawi saying that she appreciated the invitation but did not feel it proper to come. Dejected, he thought, She must have no interest in me at all!

Then a week later a beautiful hand-knit sweater arrived in the mail, with a note indicating her wish that he would visit Shillong before returning to America.

Oh, how he wanted to visit Shillong! He had never wanted to travel to any city so badly. But how could he? He had already agreed to take a month-long tour of the interior villages, beginning in Lakhipur on November 10. That would last until just before Christmas. And he was to return to the United States in January. There was just no way.

Then a letter came from the Translation Secretary of the Bible Society in Bangalore, inviting him to a Bible translators' conference in Shillong November 6–9. Could he come? It seemed a miracle. "Thank you, Lord," he said gratefully.

When Ro arrived at the Pinewood Hotel in Shillong the desk clerk told him some students were planning a reception in his honor in the Morello Tea Room. He went expectantly to the tea, but Rimawi wasn't there. Troubled, he hurried to St. Mary's College as soon as the tea was over, but the gates were already closed. He stood there in the flickering shadows, looking through the bars at the dormitory. So near and yet so far.

He returned the next day and asked for her. Taking a seat in the austere parlor, he waited impatiently.

An eternity later—actually only a few minutes—he caught sight of a beautiful young girl wearing a tribal cloth and a white embroidered blouse approaching. He rose to his feet in recognition.

She smiled shyly and his heart skipped a beat.

This is the one, he told himself intuitively. I just *know* this is the one.

They were allowed "five to ten minutes" together by the nuns but stretched it to an hour. As they talked, Ro felt that here was a girl he could fully trust. In just two months he would be ten thousand miles away, and the thought of leaving this soft-voiced, sensitive girl tore at his heart.

I must be bold and trust her to understand, he decided, and quickly declared, "I came to see if you might be God's choice for me."

He caught the surprise that flickered in her eyes and in the coloring of her delicate cheeks.

"I will be leaving the country in January. Please pray about it."

"Yes," she whispered sweetly. "I will pray."

"Please pray *soon*. The time is so short."

Rimawi suddenly dropped her eyes.

Have I spoken too hastily? Ro wondered.

Then she looked up, and her soft smile seemed to float toward him. "We have talked far past the time."

Ro glanced at his watch. The time had flown. "Do you mind," he asked in leaving, "if I called you Mawii [meaning 'beautiful one']? It is so appropriate."

She blushed in approval.

That evening they saw each other again, this time in the company of Thangkhupvung Buongpui, the guardian who had been appointed by Rimawi's brother. Again the time rushed by, and Ro had to say good-bye.

The next day he was busy at the translators' conference, but he made time for his pressing personal business. In keeping with custom, he discussed a possible marriage with a distant cousin who happened to be in town. Nor did he forget the Hmar custom of sending messages; he wrote warm, encouraging letters to Mawii during free minutes.

"I would be the happiest man in this hemisphere if our loving Father would join the two of us to one," he said in one. The messengers returned to report that she was "definitely praying over the matter" and would give him an answer on Sunday.

It was their first real date, and Ro took her canoeing on Ward Lake in front of the hotel. The sky had never seemed clearer, the sun brighter, or the water clearer as he paddled rhythmically over the smooth water.

Blind to the curious onlookers on shore, she read to him from *Tlangchar Tuihnar (This Mountain Spring)*, the devotional book he had written. The words sounded so pleasant and captivating that he could hardly believe he had written them himself.

Finally he could hold back no longer, for his heart was about to burst. "Will you marry me?" he implored.

Mawii put down the book and spoke slowly, carefully. "I have been praying about it, and even as I prayed I found myself praising the Lord for having brought about this miracle. Long years ago when I saw you at the school, I prayed that if I were ever to marry it would be to someone like Rochunga. I wanted to marry a man who loved God as you do, but I never thought it possible that it would be you.

"Now I see how the Lord has worked his plan to bring us together, and I will be happy to be your wife."

The next step was to inform their parents. Ro sent a telegram Monday morning to his mother and father at Sielmat saying, BEING IN THE WAY, THE LORD LED ME. LETTER FOLLOWS.

As he left Shillong in the evening he felt for the first time the bittersweet ache of romantic loneliness. But his heart was full and satisfied. He had found *the* girl, and she had said yes.

The tour of villages began in Lakhipur, where Ro's older brother, Ramlien, was pastor. After the Hmar custom, Ro sent Ramlien and a brother-in-law to Khawlien village where Rimawi's parents lived. They carried a blue and white cloth to signify a pleasant home and a hoe as an instrument of peace. They were to obtain from Ramawi's parents their permission for her to marry Ro and then take the news to him in Senvon.

Ramlien must have understood his brother's anxious desire to know, for he sent a flashlight signal across the valley from Khawlien saying, WE ARE SUCCESSFUL!

CHAPTER 10

Great Is God's Faithfulness

At 4 P.M. on New Year's day, 1959, Ro was standing near the altar of the William Carey Baptist Church watching his bride float down the aisle toward him.

She glanced his way and smiled. Their eyes locked. She looks like a queen, he thought. My beautiful Hmar bride!

Mawii took her place at his side. The colorful Hmar traditional wedding dress and white brocade blouse and veil accented her oriental complexion.

Ro's thoughts were whirling as Pastor Corlett spoke the solemn words of the marriage ceremony. When he paused, Ro realized it was time for him to say, "I do." Then he listened as Mawii's soft, clear voice repeated the words.

"I do."

She's mine! Ro thought as the pastor declared, "I now pronounce you man and wife." A reception was held in the church gardens. The church members, who had known Ro as a student, showered them with good wishes. They spent their wedding night at the Baptist Mission home.

The next day the newlyweds entrained for Madras, where Ro spoke at the Asian Christian Youth Congress. From there they traveled to Vellore for the Post-Congress Crusade at the famous medical training center.

Ro was introduced as "a great honeymoon preacher and

original thinker." He felt more like a honeymoon breaker. He wished it could have been possible to take his bride on a romantic trip alone somewhere, perhaps to see the Taj Mahal. But he was pleased at her gracious attitude. They not only loved each other but both loved their Lord and wished to serve him.

From Vellore they traveled to Sielmat, where he presented his new bride to his family. Daii beamed as he told her how they had followed Hmar custom, and how beautifully suited they were to one another in God's service.

"You are truly what we call *pathien samsui,*" his mother said, using the Hmar expression meaning "those who God tied together by the hair."

Mawii was especially pleased and surprised when her seventy-five-year-old father arrived after walking through rugged jungles for five days.

"Your brothers told me Rochunga was a good man and would make you a fine husband, but I wanted to see with my own eyes," her beloved father told her. "It is very hard for your mother and me to think of our youngest child going to the far side of the world where we may never see her again."

Ro was touched by the dear man's love for his daughter and explained their plans for the future. "Since Mawii's I.A. examinations are not going to be held until February, we have postponed our departure to America. We will have time to come to your village so Mawii can tell her mother good-bye."

"That will please her very much," said his father-in-law, smiling. "We will have a celebration, and you can meet all your new relatives."

When Ro and Mawii arrived in Khawlien a few weeks later they found a big feast prepared in their honor. Mawii was thrilled to receive the chest her parents had had made for her, filled with beautiful handwoven cloths, as she had given most of her Hmar cloth blouses to Ro's relatives, according to the Hmar custom. Ro was particularly impressed with his new brother-in-law, Khuma, who had been studying for his master's degree at Allahabad.

"I'm planning on entering government service after I finish my master's dissertation," Khuma explained to Ro.

"Why not come and help us start the new Christian high school?" Ro invited. "We really need you. And you could work on your dissertation in your spare time while serving as principal of the new school."

Khuma agreed, and when they arrived back in Sielmat he began planning the curriculum and looking for teachers. Ro worked with his brother-in-law a few days and then set about starting nine village schools, including one in Khawlien. Only the lack of funds kept him from establishing more.

The time soon came for Mawii to take her exams. A passing grade was required for her to receive credit for her two years of college work. She was a little apprehensive, since she had not been studying much since her marriage. Ro accompanied her to Imphal, and when the results of the examinations were announced he swelled with pride. "Why, you did better than I!" he exclaimed.

It was a joyous occasion for Ro when he said, "My wife, Mawii" to Watkin Roberts at the Toronto airport. Mr. Young Man took her to his heart as a daughter and insisted they stay a few days before continuing on to Chicago.

When they reached Wheaton, Ro enjoyed introducing his bride to all his friends. It seemed so natural and pleasant to have her with him. It was as if a void in his life had now been filled.

Mawii was very impressed by the friendly, open, frank Americans. She was a little shy about her English, even though everyone encouraged her. The church services were a special blessing to her, after years of only private devotions in a Catholic college. The common bond of their love for the Lord made her feel right at home.

Ro and Mawii worked together getting out their first prayer letter. Ro had it mimeographed at an office in Wheaton, and then the two of them hand-addressed the envelopes. Putting the letters in the mail was a special thrill. They had begun their work for the mission.

One day Ro dropped by to see a board member, radio preacher John D. Jess of the Chapel of the Air. He reported to Jess the progress among the Hmars and the enthusiasm of the tribal church leaders to start more schools and build a strong mission base. "With nationals telling other nationals," Ro declared, "all of northeast India can be evangelized. I must enlist the help of all the Christians in the United States," he added optimistically.

"How are you going to get around to see everybody?" Jess grinned.

"I'll start with two strong legs!" Ro replied.

"Those legs won't take you very far. This is a big country."

Ro's eyes shone with determination. "They are strong enough. I will walk from house to house until I have knocked on the door of every home in Wheaton, if necessary. Then I'll go to Glen Ellyn and Lombard and—"

"Whoa. Why don't you let me put a little speed to your faith? Go over to Madsen's used car lot and pick out any vehicle you wish. I'll pay for it."

Excited as a schoolboy, Ro dashed down to the lot and put his hands on a gleaming white late-model Plymouth. "Lord, is this the one?" he prayed. No answer.

He moved to another and did the same. Again, no answer.

Finally he prayed over an old 1952 Mercury, and every pulse that beat within him seemed to say, *Yours! Yours!*

By this time the manager had noticed the strange foreigner feeling his cars. "What are you doing?" he demanded.

"I'm looking at my car!" Ro replied straightforwardly.

"Your car?"

"This one. What is the price?"

"Only two seventy-five. It has a beautiful engine."

"I will give two hundred."

"No."

"Two twenty-five. Not a penny more."

"Take it!"

"I'll get the money. How shall the check be made out?"

Jess was surprised that Ro had picked out one of the cheapest cars on the lot, but Ro insisted it was the one God wanted him to have. Jess gave him the check, helped with the papers, and Ro was on his way home.

Ro then rented a small upstairs room (twelve feet by six feet) on Main Street for $25 a month and opened the Indo-Burma Pioneer Mission's first U.S. office. Here he compiled in a black and white composition book the mission's first mailing list—114 names. Funds began trickling in as a result of their first mailing.

Mawii enrolled in summer school and Ro hit the road, driving over ten thousand miles across the Midwest in the Mercury that summer. He presented a new concept in missions that captured the imaginations of laymen: *partnership between Americans and nationals.*

"I am not antimissionary," he insisted. "A missionary—Watkin Roberts—brought the gospel to our tribe. But then he had to go away, leaving the first Hmar believers to evangelize their own people, build their own churches, educate their own children.

"Everyone knows that the day of the foreign missionary in India is fading. Americans are no longer allowed in as missionary preachers and teachers. The foreign force drops steadily while population and nationalistic feelings increase. "Most members of our tribe are now Christians. We have hundreds of young men and women willing to become missionaries themselves to other tribes. But we are poor and unable to train and send all of them.

"Remember, a national does not need passage money. He is already there. He does not need expensive equipment or language training. He speaks the language and is acquainted with the customs of the people. He cannot be expelled, for he is not a foreigner.

"So we ask for your financial partnership in our program of nationals training and telling nationals. Ten dollars will pay the tuition of a Bible college student for one month; forty dollars will support a pastor or evangelist; one hundred dollars will operate an entire village school; one thousand dollars will build a two-room school."

Wherever Ro spoke, he asked for the names and addresses of those who showed interest in the partnership program of the mission. These were added to the fast-growing mailing list.

Late in the summer he was struck in Iowa by the "civilized disease" of hay fever. It got so bad that sometimes he had to stop in the middle of a sermon, duck behind the pulpit, and spray his nostrils to keep breathing. The sneezing and wheezing, runny nose, and itching eyes plagued him until after the first frost.

By this time the "secret" that is unmentionable in Hmar society was apparent, and Mawii didn't enroll for the fall semester. Ro was ecstatic at the prospect of fatherhood. How had he ever stood the lonely life of a bachelor? His greatest loneliness now came on weekends when Mawii was unable to accompany him on a speaking trip.

While it was still dark on November 1, Mawii whispered urgently, "My time has come." The old Mercury got her to the hospital at 7:30 A.M., and at 9:04 their howling, red-faced son was born. Ro gazed at the wiggly newborn baby with great awe.

The enchanted parents named him Paul Rozarlien. They felt he should have both a biblical name and a Hmar name. All in all, 1959 had been quite a year! In India Ro had acquired a wife and started nine new schools; in America, a car, an office, and now a son! And he had barnstormed the Midwest, stirring up interest in India. How well he had done was revealed in the mission's first audit: it showed $9,643.90 in receipts.

He began the new decade with unbounded enthusiasm over what God was going to accomplish. Since both he and Mawii were in the United States on student visas, they had to continue their schoolwork. But Ro's heart was more in the mission than in the classroom. He continued driving the faithful old Mercury to weekend speaking engagements.

When summer came they rigged up a bassinet in the back seat and drove to Washington, D.C., stopping at churches along the way to tell the Hmar story, making more contacts, meeting more people, adding to the mailing list. They returned to Wheaton wilted and exhausted, but warmly content in God's evident blessing.

By late summer Ro and Mawii were both exhausted, and nothing seemed to help Ro's hay fever. Antihistamine drugs only dulled his thinking.

One August night when they were back home for a brief period to catch up on written work, Mawii prayed, "Lord, Ro cannot breathe any more. Help him." But the next morning he felt as miserable as ever.

"I don't know if I can last another day," he said. "I wish I could disappear somewhere until the frost. I can't even think straight."

He went to pick up the mail from the post office box.

There was one personal letter, from a couple named Anderson, and he lingered in the cool air conditioning to open it. His red, watery, bloodshot eyes widened as he read:

> Dear Ro and Mawii:
> The Faucettes were here yesterday and told us how miserable you, Ro, feel with your hay fever. We have a place here by a lake in northern Wisconsin where it will not bother you. Come and be with us for this week and next. The cabin is free.

What an answer to prayer! There was no way they could have afforded a vacation on Ro's $200 monthly salary, and now it was being offered to them free of charge.

They left the next morning, but Ro was so exhausted from sneezing all night that 400 miles seemed like an endless journey. They stopped constantly to put in eye drops.

By the time they reached Fond du Lac, Ro was ready to give up and just stay there to suffer. "But think of the joy of sleeping tonight without sneezing," Mawii whispered encouragingly. "The tall pines will sing us songs of heaven. And we can go rowing in their little boat. Come on, let me put the drops in one more time."

He consented and they drove on. As they came to Eagle River, Ro's nose "miraculously" opened and his eyes stopped itching. They arrived at the Andersons to find a delicious fish dinner awaiting them. It was the first meal Ro had really enjoyed in weeks. He ate and ate.

The Andersons then walked them to a hilltop guest cabin shaded by tall pines. They slept on an innerspring mattress on the floor. It was so relaxing.

The next two weeks Ro studied the Bible and prayed every day, and the rest of the time they hiked through the deep woods, picking blueberries or just enjoying the solemnity of the whispering forest. Baby Paul bumped along on their backs, snug in a Hmar *puon* scarf, gurgling his delight.

The respite in the pines refreshed their spirits, and they returned to Illinois with new zest. Mawii enrolled again at Wheaton, with Ro transferring to Northern Illinois University, a seventy-mile round trip each day. He had decided that a master's degree in education from a secular university would be more beneficial than a degree in theology.

The British and Foreign Bible Society cabled in December that the Hmar New Testaments were coming off the presses. A few days later Ro's special translator's copy arrived. As he reverently patted the black buckram cover, his mind swept back across the years. Tears welled in his eyes as he heard his father saying, "You know that Ramlien, our oldest, will receive the inheritance along with the responsibility of caring for us in our old age. You are free to get the education that will fit you for the task of translation. Our people need it so badly. We know that with God's help you can do it." And his mother vowing, "My hands will take the hoe until you receive your B.A. degree!"

"Lord, thank you for giving me such good parents and such a kind loving wife," he said. "Thank you for providing and keeping me on the right path. Thank you for this Book and all who helped make it possible. Make it an instrument of your Spirit for the enlightening of my people."

Two weeks later he was leading a seminar discussion at the university when a receptionist opened the door. "Is there a man here named Pudaite? He has a son just born at the hospital in St. Charles."

Ro wrapped up the discussion with as much decorum

as he could muster and sped to Mawii's bedside. Labor had
started after he had left. She had called the doctor, who
had come by for her, leaving a friend to take care of
Paul. Ro was proud and amazed at how calmly she had
handled everything in the birth of John Lalnunsang
Pudaite.

After getting Paul to bed that night, Ro was too full of
emotion to sleep. He sat reading his Bible, praying, and
meditating on God's blessings. The Lord had given him a
sweet, loving wife who was a joy to work with, and she
had given him two fine sons. The growth of the work
was a joy, too. The number of village schools had doubled.
The high school and Bible Institute enrollments had increased. The recent audit showed that $40,971.17 had been
contributed by American "partners" during 1960. God was
very good.

CHAPTER 11

Growing Pains

The news struck Hmar land like lightning announcing the end of a long drought. "The Bibles are here!"

At last the printed New Testaments had arrived from London, crates and crates of precious hardbound copies. There were ten thousand in the first printing.

Thousands of Hmars gathered at the Sielmat headquarters for a joyous feast of thanksgiving and to receive their first precious books. This was followed by a special day of dedication observed in every village. No one was prouder than Chawnga, whose only regret was that his son could not be present to see the joy in the readers' faces.

The new Christian bookstore in Sielmat did a landslide business. Within six months, by the summer of 1961, the first printing was sold out. An order for ten thousand more copies went to Bangalore, where the Bible Society had sent the plates. But there was bad news as well. Word came that the walls of the new high school building were up but no roofing materials were available anywhere. The monsoons would soon come. What should they do?

In desperation Ro explained the problem to his good friend John Jess. "What if you don't get the roof up before it rains?" the broadcaster asked.

"We'll have the biggest built-in swimming pool in all Asia," Ro replied sadly. Jess prayed for Ro.

Raising support for the growing work was a continuing problem. The number of evangelistic workers had passed one hundred, each requiring $25 monthly. One month they were $40 short when time came to mail the check. Ro put off mailing it as long as he could, praying the Lord would provide, so the poorly paid workers would not have to go without.

Two hours later a young friend, John Arnold, stopped by on his lunch break. He pulled an envelope from his overall pocket and handed it to Ro. "For the work in India," he said. The envelope contained four ten-dollar bills.

Most of the support came from such people. An Illinois widow sent 25 cents per month. A woman in South Dakota fasted during Easter week and gave 25 cents a meal to the tribal mission. A thirteen-year-old California girl sent $1 at a time from baby-sitting wages. An Iowa teen-ager sold greeting cards and sent a tithe of his income. A pastor and his wife in Norfolk, Virginia, estimated they would spend $57 for Christmas and sent half that amount.

In India the Hmar Christians gave as they could to the missions outreach. Farmers gave a tithe of their crops. Church boxes were placed on every trail leading into villages. Women carrying firewood dropped one stick from each load into the box. When full, the contents were sold and the proceeds given to the church.

When Mawii's brother, Khuma, came to Wheaton College Graduate School and later to Moody Bible Institute for further study, the direction in the field was left to the capable Lalthankun Sinate. Ro was encouraged to realize that more and more tribesmen were becoming well educated and trained for leadership. Lal's widowed mother and sister had worked in the rice fields and also woven cloth so that he might finish high school. Then, after graduation from the Union Biblical Seminary at Yeotmal, he had come into the work. Khuma and Lal were Ro's two most trusted lieutenants. Either one, he felt, was capable of holding the work together in India.

When Ro's long-time dream of a Christian college among the Hmars was about to be fulfilled, dependable Khuma returned to Sielmat to become the principal. The chief problem, he reported back to Ro, was in securing a qualified faculty. He was finally forced to hire several non-Christian instructors.

While reading the mail one morning shortly afterward, Ro let out a deep sigh. "What's wrong, darling?" Mawii was always quick to sense Ro's moods. "You sound discouraged."

"Oh, I have here a report from Lal. He says the directors of the Hmar church are complaining that I hold 'dictatorial powers' since I serve as both executive director of the mission and as head of the Hmar church. They want a new constitution that would separate the church from the mission society."

"But Ro, that shows our people are maturing. Isn't this what you have wanted and planned for?"

"Yes, I am thrilled that the national church will soon be able to administer its own institutions and workers. And I believe that a new constitution might be just the thing to encourage this emerging spirit of independence the people are showing. I just want the changeover to go smoothly and without friction.

"You know, Mawii, I was just thinking. It's been five years since we left India. Perhaps this would be a good time for us to take a furlough."

"A—a furlough? You mean we would go home to India!" Mawii exclaimed as the import of his words registered with her. "Ro, could we really go home?"

"Yes, I believe the timing is perfect. Things are running smoothly here, and we are needed there to help in this transition period. And we will be able to take Paul and Johnny with us to see our homeland and meet their grandparents."

"Oh, Ro. I am so-o-o-o happy!" And Mawii threw her arms around him in an impetuous hug.

Shortly before they were to leave for India, Mawii was invited to a luncheon at the Wheaton Free Church. There she presented the need for a Hmar hospital. The church already had a large missionary budget, but the women persuaded the pastor and the mission committee to authorize them to raise funds for the hospital's first building. This was just the kind of news they needed to take back to India.

The Hmars greeted their arrival with a huge reception where all their friends and relatives gathered to greet them. Paul and Johnny were the center of attraction. The four- and five-year-olds ate up the affection lavished upon them by grandparents, aunts, and uncles. They were soon playing with their many cousins and picking up Hmar words rapidly.

Soon after the Pudaites arrived, Laltuoklien, the medical student Ro had helped support for so long, received his M.B.B.S. As the first qualified Hmar doctor, he agreed to take over the planned hospital.

Ro spent most of the six-month stay traveling. He visited as many of the remote villages as possible, talking, planning, counseling the people, and encouraging them to become more independent.

Mawii was especially happy to have time with her widowed mother. "My mother, I have a special secret to share with you," Mawii told her softly. "We are going to have another child. Ro and I would like you to name this baby."

Her aging mother spent a few minutes in silent contemplation. "The name is Lalsangpui," she announced. " 'The Lord is supremely great.' "

Ro wanted to stay for the July church assembly, when new leaders would be elected in line with the new constitution, but he felt they should return to the United States. Donations had dropped in his absence. The time had passed so quickly, it was hard to bid farewell to their loved ones again.

From Wheaton Ro mailed in his resignation as president of the church, but to his surprise he was nominated again and returned to office. The church did agree to take over the bookstore, the preparation of literature, and part of the evangelistic outreach, which Ro felt was a step in the right direction, but they wanted the mission to continue to operate the schools and the hospital and fund the national workers which the church couldn't adequately support.

When their third child was born, they gave her the biblical name of Mary and, in accordance with her grandmother's wishes, the tribal name Lalsangpui. "Mother must have known this one would be a girl," Mawii exclaimed, "for she chose no boy's name."

A few weeks later Ro hung up the phone and murmured, "The Lord gives and the Lord takes away. Well, not quite. Pu Tlangval is dying, Mawii. We must go."

Before they could leave for Canada, they had to get the consent of the immigration department. When this permission was delayed, they feared the old missionary they loved so much would die without their being able to say good-bye.

"What can we do?" Mawii wailed. "We must see him again."

"I know," Ro agreed. "Red tape can be so frustrating. But there is really nothing we can do but pray that he lives until we get there. Why don't you get the Bible and read to us?"

Johnny climbed up on his daddy's lap, and Paul snuggled close beside him while their mother read to them. Baby Mary slept through the reading.

Mawii was feeling so desolate that while she read the 78th Psalm the tears slid down her cheeks. Then when she reached Psalm 79, she stopped, looked up, and smiled. She read again the verse which said the Lord would "preserve . . . those that are appointed to die."

"Let's thank him for that assurance," Ro said and led them in a prayer of rejoicing, while the Roberts family in Canada was thinking that they would have to make funeral arrangements.

It was a whole week before travel permissions came, but they never lost faith that they would see Mr. Young Man again. When Ro finally arrived in Toronto he found Roberts sitting up in his hospital bed, smiling.

"When I heard you couldn't get here, I just decided to live a little longer," he explained. "I couldn't die without first saying good-bye to my beloved Rochunga and Mawii!"

To the doctors' amazement, he recovered completely.

CHAPTER 12
Burning Hills

The work seemed to roll along, gathering momentum as it went. The board voted to change the name to Partnership Mission, which was more in keeping with their philosophy. The months passed with Ro unaware that an insidious enemy was gnawing, termitelike, at the very foundation of the work in India.

Since the early fifties, neighboring tribes of the Hmars had been pushing for independence from India. They had asked for foreign help from Western democracies, but when it was not forthcoming one rebel leader declared, "They told us how to go to heaven, but they cannot take us to the U.N. We must now turn to the East."

Two thousand young Nagas crossed into China to receive guerrilla training. Their return in 1967 shook the mountains of northeast India. The government in New Delhi declared the entire area "sensitive" and off limits to foreign visitors.

Because the Hmars were loyal to the Indian government, they became prime targets for subversion. Slowly, quietly, undercover agents worked themselves into positions of respect and influence in Hmar society.

Meanwhile Ro and Mawii were busy establishing a program named Partnership Parents to support native children, starving as the result of a great famine. Hmar Christians opened their hearts and homes to these pitiful little ones who were brought in desperation to the mission office in Sielmat. American "foster parents" supplied the funds, $12 monthly for each child, to provide housing, food, clothing, education, medical care, and Bible instruction.

While political rebellion was brewing among the students of the college, the Pudaites were rejoicing in the reports of progress coming from the hospital. The twenty-five-bed facility with seven staff members assisting the one doctor was meeting the needs of patients who formerly had only pagan priests with tribal remedies to turn to.

One Hmar chief was not only healed but became a Christian and went home rejoicing in Christ. Another patient was a young boy near death who amazingly recovered after the removal of a 45-foot tapeworm. A woman in labor for a week was carried in on a stretcher. The staff delivered the baby and sent mother and child home healthy and strong.

"Our biggest problem now is success," Ro mused naïvely one evening at the dinner table. "The college needs more buildings. The hospital is crying for enlargement. It seems a never-ending spiral."

Then the foundations began to crumble. Khuma did not think it wise even to report on paper all that was happening. Instead he summed up the pleas of the Hmar loyalists by imploring Ro to come home.

The entire family responded to Khuma's call of distress. Ro, Mawii, Paul, John, and even three-year-old Mary got on the plane for India.

In November Khuma and Chawnga met them at the Imphal airport with distressing news. "Communist propaganda has the campus in an uproar," the younger man said. "False stories have been spread all over the area about you." Ro was a CIA agent, said the stories. He had smuggled five million dollars into the country; why didn't he share it with the people? He had brought in arms and ammunition to the China-Burma borders.

The tales were ridiculous, but how could he convince those who had been duped? Then the letters started coming. "If you don't leave India, we will hang you upside down behind your house," one threatened. "You will never leave Manipur on two feet," another warned. "You'll be skinned alive so that you feel pain until the moment you expire," said still another. There were twenty-nine such letters in all.

Ro's rented car was stoned four times, and the authorities warned him not to drive at night.

Once he was caught by darkness only two miles from Sielmat. He had with him a Christian tribesman and felt he must take him down a side road as far toward his village as he could drive. On the way he passed eight men armed with automatic weapons lurking by the roadside. He knew they would be waiting in ambush as he returned.

Ro dropped his passenger where the road dead-ended at a river crossing and turned back. Nearing the place of expected ambush, he crouched low and jammed the accelerator to the floor. As he sped by, the men threw rocks but did not fire their weapons.

Clearly Ro had become a marked man. Two weeks later he received information that over a hundred armed men were surrounding his house, boasting they would kill him before the night was over. He reported the danger to the police, but they said it would take several hours to gather a force large enough to protect him. Fearing for the lives of his family, Ro drove home through the darkness with headlights off, parked before the door, and ran inside.

There he saw Mawii, Ramlien, his parents, and the children having devotions. They had not been aware of the men outside. As Ro joined them, little Mary began singing, "I Trust in God Wherever I May Be." Then they prayed for God's guidance and for their enemies.

The long night passed without any attempt at forced entry. They were wondering what had happened to the men when Khuma arrived. "When I learned you couldn't get enough police help," he said, "I organized our friends to protect you. They didn't dare attack."

Three more times the house was surrounded by would-be attackers. Each time loyal friends, with the help of local police, prevented violence.

When the authorities got everything under control, Ro and Mawii prepared to return to Wheaton. Before leaving, Ro spoke to an assembly of Hmars. "We must forgive our enemies," he implored. "Let us seek reconciliation with those who were deceived by the political agitators."

He then set the example by going to the jail and asking the release of those charged with his attempted murder. "They were merely the pawns of ringleaders who have fled," he told the officials. "We still love them and forgive them. Please let them go. When they learn the whole truth, they will be for us."

An official investigation of the whole affair was conducted by the federal government. The final report stated, "We've never seen any group accomplish so much with so little. Carry on!"

In April, 1969, a call came to Ro in Wheaton from Ruth Roberts. "Dad is dying, Ro."

"Are they certain?"

"Yes. I believe it is his time. He has developed shingles, besides his other complications. He's having a lot of pain. He's ready to go."

"You know we will miss him terribly, Ruth. But we will pray his passing will be easy."

When word came a few days later that he was gone, there was no anguish. The Pudaite family went to Toronto for the simple services, attended by the family and a few intimate friends, in accordance with Watkin Roberts' final wishes. The services were conducted by Dr. J. Oswald Smith, with Ro briefly eulogizing the missionary pioneer who had meant so much to his tribe. The rites were much like the great missionary statesman had been, dignified, spiritual, and uplifting.

Ro and Mawii felt the finest way to pay tribute to his memory was to continue the work he had loved so much. During the summer of 1970 they started something new. The entire family was on the road for twelve thousand miles through seventeen states. On this itinerary they cooked and served "thank you" Indian dinners to hundreds and hundreds of their loyal supporters.

In August Mawii left the children with Ro and went to India to work for the Partnership Parents' homes and to organize the Sielmat Christian Hospital Women's Auxiliary. She found the hospital overcrowded with patients.

Dr. Thangkhum and his dedicated staff were treating over eight hundred people each month. The outpatient room was so crowded that she could scarcely find room to stand. The seriously ill patients of both sexes were jammed into one barracks-type ward. The need for another wing, especially for women patients, was apparent.

While Mawii was away, Ro took the three children to Wisconsin for a short vacation. They had driven only about a hundred miles when their little VW jolted to a stop. A tow truck had to pull them twenty miles to the nearest garage, where they waited a day and night for a report. Then the mechanic told them that repairs might take two more days.

It was a discouraging experience. Ro didn't know how he would keep the children happy cooped up in a motel room. Should they return to Wheaton on the bus? Or just wait for the car?

He gathered the children around him to pray. When it was Mary's turn, she said, "Dear God, we don't want to stay here. My brothers want to catch fish, and I want to catch fish. Why don't you do something, God?"

When they finished, Ro called the manager of the local

VW agency and explained their predicament. "Come right
over," he invited, "and I'll lend you a new car to take up
north. Your car will be ready on your way back."
It was as simple as that. They were fishing before sundown. When they returned their car was ready and the
VW manager wouldn't charge a cent for rental. Ro learned
never to doubt a child's faith.

When the regular board meeting was held at the end of
the year, Ro had a glowing report to give.
"Nineteen seventy has proved to be our best year to
date," he told the members as they ate lunch together.
"Gifts were up over forty percent from the previous year.
From one hundred forty-seven thousand dollars to over
two hundred and eleven thousand.
"Our field reports show the mission is now supporting
three hundred fifty national missionaries. We have sixty-
five village schools operating, in addition to the Christian
high school and the hospital.
"As you know, the college has been closed since the
unrest, but Khuma hopes it will soon be reopened.
"Twelve new churches have been started in Manipur
and Assam with over two thousand converts. Besides this,
a half million tracts and a quarter million Gospels of John
have been distributed among the hill tribes."
Then, just when the future seemed brightest, a new
challenge came in January from political leaders in Ro's
home state. "The Communist who has represented Manipur in Parliament has no chance of being reelected," they
said. "The government investigation showed the people
who their true friends are. If you will come and file as our
candidate, we can assure your election."
Ro leaned across Mawii's desk with a big smile. "Read
this," he said, handing her the letter. He watched as her
brows raised and her eyes rounded in wonder.

"Oh, Ro!" she exclaimed. "How marvelous!"

"Yes," he agreed. "I wonder what our board would think of my being a Member of Parliament?"

"What? But—but you aren't really considering doing it, are you? We'd have to give up our work here and return to India."

"Well, I could at least think about it," Ro said thoughtfully. "A Member of Parliament. Why, I gave up on that dream years ago."

To Mawii's chagrin Ro began asking for different opinions. He talked privately with each of the board members. Everyone encouraged him. It seemed such a great opportunity.

"But Ro," Mawii protested, "you already have the most important job in the world—serving the Lord Jesus."

"Don't you see, Mawii, how this could advance the work of the mission? It would give it more status. I could involve the government in some of our projects, and I could be a Christian witness on the floor of Parliament. Why, I could even help other mission groups working in India."

"I'm sorry, darling, but it seems to be a sidetrack. Here we are making all these plans for a campaign to reach Imphal with the gospel, and you want to go off politicking!"

She turned from him and ran from the office to their home nearby. Up in her bedroom she knelt and prayed while the tears flowed. "Lord, help me to understand. Give me peace about this matter. Ro seems so enthusiastic, and I should be an encouragement to him."

That night Ro wrestled with the problem. He appreciated Mawii's feelings but knew the decision had to be his. He prayed much of the night, asking the Lord to show him the right path. "Help me not to consider any ambitions of my own but only to be willing to follow wherever you lead."

Before the night was over, he had his answer. This opportunity had to be of the Lord; it was too fantastic to have just happened. To try to make Mawii see how clearly this seemed of the Lord, he put down in writing his reasons for the decision.

He tiptoed upstairs and placed the letter beside her sleeping form. When she awoke the next morning and read it, her tears began to flow again. "Give me confidence, Lord, that you are leading Ro," she prayed.

At the breakfast table Ro discussed the decision with the children. The normally wiggly, noisy threesome realized the importance of what their father was saying and listened respectfully.

But Mawii was still crying. The tears streamed down her face. She sniffled and blew her nose until finally Paul said, "Mommy, we can't hear what Daddy is saying!"

"Oh, I am so sorry, Ro," she apologized.

Ro went over to his beloved wife and placed his arms around her comfortingly. "Sweetheart, just think what an opportunity this will be to show the rest of India what Christianity has done for our tribe. Certainly this will hold back the rising flood of resentment against missionaries. Don't you want to go back home?"

"Oh, Ro, you know how much I would love to live in India again. I just don't want to do anything to displease the Lord."

"I'll pray he will give you peace about this decision as he has me."

Ro prepared to leave, taking a flight scheduled to arrive two days before the filing deadline. All went well until the plane landed for refueling at Tashkent airport on the southern tip of Russia. The pilot first announced they would be on the ground for only twenty-five minutes; then he said there would be a delay for repairs and the passengers should go to a hotel.

It was 25 degrees below zero outside, and the hotel

room was unheated. Ro shivered in his topcoat underneath a single blanket and sheet while his assigned roommate got drunk and vomited all over the bed. The plane
finally left the next afternoon and arrived in New Delhi
fifteen minutes past the deadline for filing.

Khuma and several leaders were still waiting at the airport. Khuma was as crushed as Ro, but nothing could be
done. The two climbed wearily into a taxi and went to a
hotel. Exhausted, they tried to pray for understanding before succumbing to sleep.

Ro was so disconsolate that he couldn't even talk about
the crushing turn of events. But he must tell the news to
Mawii and his children, so he sent a cable to them right
away. The message came to Mawii in the mission office.
Her first reaction was, How very disappointed he must be!
Without even explaining to the other workers, she ran
home to her bedside to pray for him.

"The Lord must have a purpose in this," Ro kept assuring
himself and others who shared his disappointment. With
this thought in mind he and Khuma left for Imphal, where
Hmar church leaders had planned a saturation crusade in
witnessing. The city of 300,000, with 200,000 more within
a five-mile radius, did not have a single church, nor had
any foreigner ever been permitted to preach there.

Five hundred Hmar lay workers had volunteered to
serve on the team. But since there were only buses for 320,
those under fifteen and over fifty were asked to remain in
Sielmat to pray for the meetings. The 320 took along
150,000 copies of John 3:1–16 in the Manipuri language,
the most widely spoken in Imphal, and within three hours
gave them all away.

During the crusade, Ro's brother Ramlien brought a
Muslim teacher to Ro's room. "This is Mr. Renchang
Chote. He wishes to debate with you," Ramlien explained.

Ro looked at his watch. He hadn't much time. "Very

well," he said. "Let's do it the way they do in the United
States. You take ten minutes and tell me all Mohammed has
done for you that you're excited about, and I'll take ten
minutes to tell what Jesus has done for me. Then I must
go speak."

"You begin," the man with the flowing black robe and
beard suggested courteously.

"No, you are my guest," Ro replied. "You may go first."

"No, I insist that you tell me first."

"Very well," Ro acquiesced. "As you know, I am a
tribal man. My grandfather was a headhunter, and my
father was trained to be one. But God changed my father
from being a headhunter to being a heart-hunter for Jesus
Christ. It was because of the power of God.

"I too have received this experience of having Christ
in my heart. Since I became Christian I have been so sure
of God's leadership I never have to worry about what is
done to me today or tomorrow. I know I have a home in
heaven.

"Jesus Christ has met every need of my life. There have
been times when I had a terrible need for money for my
own support when I was in school. He supplied all I needed.
There were times when I was in danger of losing my life
in the jungle. Wild animals chased me, but when I turned
my needs over to Jesus Christ he met every one of them.

"The most exciting thing about life is that when you
know the source of joy and peace and light and life, then
you have everything. That I have. For all these reasons
and more, I am just bubbling over with joy.

"Now it is your turn," Ro said, glancing quickly at his
watch.

The Muslim moved uneasily, looked at Ro, then at
the floor.

"It's your time," Ro urged politely.

"No," he said, shaking his head. "I have nothing like that

to tell. I surrender my time. Will you take my ten minutes
and tell me how Jesus can help me?"

Ro needed no urging. In ten minutes he had told of
God's love and how Jesus had died to save men from
their sins.

Then the Muslim asked, "May I have Jesus in my heart?"
They knelt together and prayed, and Ro left to preach.

Just as he went to the rostrum, Ro noticed Ramlien and
the Muslim entering the auditorium. "Would you tell everyone what happened this morning?" Ro asked the man.

The black-robed spiritual leader stepped to the front,
looked around, and declared, "I went to debate Mr.
Pudaite, but instead I received Jesus Christ as my Savior."

After the crusade the new converts were invited to a
thirty-day course on basic Bible doctrines taught in Sielmat
by Khuma. Many came at the price of persecution and rejection by their families. One of the keenest was Renchang Chote, now a humble follower of Jesus Christ. The
former Muslim scholar, who had been trained in Persian,
Arabic, English, and Hebrew, stated that he wished to
become a minister.

Ro was convinced now that the Lord had a purpose in
his missing the political opportunity. He flew back to
Wheaton with fresh ambition to advance the ministry of
the mission over a wider area.

CHAPTER 13

Bibles for the World!

Ro's heart continued to burn with the desire to reach the world for Christ. He was acutely conscious that after two millenniums an estimated half of the world's population still had not even heard the name of Jesus—and some three hundred million of these were in India.

He did some research and ascertained that it would take a team of four thousand missionaries a thousand years to speak just once to everyone in India about Christ—provided the population didn't continue to grow at its present rate of more than a million a month. The solution had to lie with national leadership: teachers, doctors, lawyers, government officials. But these were the very people who were not being reached. It was no secret that Christianity in India had found its greatest appeal among the lowest castes. These converts were contemptuously called "rice Christians" by the upper classes.

The burden lingered into summer. Ro spent hours on his knees beseeching God to reveal a new method, some means by which he might accomplish the task which the Western-dominated church had failed to complete.

One day in July his concentration kept being broken by the telephone company jingle, "Let your fingers do the walking." In frustration he stopped praying.

As he rose from his knees, his eyes caught two telephone directories on his desk. Suddenly the vision was clear.

Those books listed the names and addresses of everyone in Calcutta and New Delhi wealthy enough to afford telephones—the best educated, most influential people, the very leaders he wanted to reach.

That's it! he thought. We'll mail the Gospel! There are over a million telephone subscribers in India, and 98 percent of them know English. We'll mail New Testaments in modern English and reach the previously unreachable. Coming from an Indian, they won't reject God's Word as foreign propaganda.

Why, by letting our fingers do the walking, we could reach the whole world. The Word of God in the language of the people has always been the best missionary. Paperbacks would keep the cost down. But they'd have to be clear, large type with a sharp cover.

Bibles for the whole world? Will the board think I'm crazy? Perhaps they will, but if the vision is from God, surely he will prepare the way.

He shared the idea with Mawii, who was working on the current newsletter. Seeing her eyes light up, he hugged her affectionately.

A few days later Dr. Kenneth Taylor, the paraphraser of *The Living Bible*, called. "Ro, we're preparing to work with the World Home Bible League in printing some *Living New Testaments* for Asian distribution. I'd like your opinion on what the artists have done for a cover picture."

Ro was flattered. It wasn't often that an American asked his opinion on something. "I'll be right over," he said.

"Oh, no." Taylor laughed. "I'm the one asking a favor. I'll come to your office."

The tall, slim Bible scholar arrived shortly and handed Ro a paperback. The cover bore the title *The Greatest Is Love* and showed a white man with a dark man on his back.

Ro swallowed hard. The same old great white father motif that has turned my people off for generations, he thought indignantly.

He looked up at his friend. "Do you really want my opinion, Ken?"

"Yes. Your frank appraisal. That's why I asked."

"Scrap it! This is a put-on. Asians know white Americans don't go around carrying blacks on their backs."

Taylor took the advice graciously. "Well, what would you suggest we use?" he asked.

"Give me five minutes to think about it," Ro replied.

Taylor went into the office kitchen and had coffee with Mawii and some of the staff. He returned to find Ro beaming.

"The Taj Mahal, Ken. The Taj is an Asian symbol of love to the whole world."

The keen-minded Taylor instantly saw Ro's wisdom. "Great. Have you got a color print we could use?"

"Yes." Ro smiled. "Mawii and I visited the Taj on our last trip, and she got some beautiful slides. I'm sure she'll go to the house and get some for you."

A couple of weeks later Taylor returned with the artists' version of the new cover.

"Beautiful! Just beautiful!" Ro enthused. Then he added, "You know, the Lord has given me a vision of making New Testaments available to many Indians through the mail. Could we use this same edition?"

"Certainly. After all, you provided the cover."

"I mean, would we have to pay royalties for use of your *Living New Testament?*"

"For paperbacks? To be given away? No, you wouldn't need to pay."

Next Ro talked with the World Home Bible League. They would be glad to print the New Testaments at cost. With no royalties to pay, Ro figured they could mail the Testaments for around a dollar each. *Only* a dollar. All the mission would have to raise to make the dream come true was $275 million, plus a dollar for each additional telephone installed before the mailing was completed.

Following the board's approval of the project, an order for 125,000 copies was placed and an appeal made to local churches for volunteers to come in and type labels, starting with the New Delhi directory.

Ro started talking it up. At a Christian Businessmen's Committee meeting of thirty to forty men, he held up one of the promotion copies and said, "If you'll buy one like this for ten dollars I'll send nine more to India." He "sold" over thirty copies on that basis.

But his exhilaration over this response was dampened by a call from the Bible League's printers. They would need $10,000 by the next week to buy paper. Since they were doing the job for cost, they felt they could not put up the money themselves.

"Well, Lord," Ro prayed, "if we get the ten thousand by next week, we'll surely know you are behind this Bible mailing. I could never raise that much money in such a short time."

On Sunday Ro shared his burden with the congregation where he was speaking. They had five minutes of silent prayer, beseeching God to intervene. Before the week was over, Ro reported back that the miracle had occurred. The money had come in.

Fueled by Ro's efforts and other promotions, the contributions continued to arrive: coins from children's piggy banks, Vacation Bible School offerings, widows' "mites," dollars from baby-sitting teen-agers and old-age pensioners, contributions from women's missionary societies.

Along with the money came scores of local volunteers to help address, stuff, and mail the Bibles. The volunteer who gave the most time was arthritic Carl Schingoethe, who worked nearly every day from the beginning of the program. "Maybe I can't walk," he quipped, "but I can serve the Lord by letting my fingers do the walking."

The first page of each *Living New Testament* included a short personal testimony from Ro with the invitation: "If

you have any question or problem concerning Jesus
Christ or how you may have peace and everlasting life
through Him, please write me." An office in New Delhi
was opened to receive mail, and letters started coming.

> This is my first experience reading the Bible. . . . I am
> a Hindu.

> Thank you for the Holy Book. Please send me other
> literature. My friend is also interested.

> I read . . . and I feel fully influenced with what the
> Bible says. I have no words to say . . . but I think I
> have reached a height where I see nothing but Christ
> who died so that we might live. No one on earth can
> shake my love for Christ. I want to know more about
> Him, about the Bible, and about myself.

> I have come to know that you have Bible in modern
> English. If it is so, kindly let me know. . . . I am a
> Muslim.

The requests for additional New Testaments had not
been anticipated, but the board decided to send them as
long as funds permitted.

An evangelical foundation then made an unprecedented
offer: to match every dollar the mission raised, in units of
$50,000, until $250,000 was received.

Ro was confident that these higher goals could be
achieved. As he demonstrated to the board with a rubber
band flexed over his short fingers: "You can stretch this
band only so far before it breaks. But the farther faith
stretches, the stronger it becomes."

And the letters kept coming:

> I am very grateful to you for sending me this sacred
> Bible. I was looking for someone who could guide me
> to such a path of brightness. I am a Sikh boy of age 23.

Thank you very much for this book, *The Greatest Is Love.* . . . This is a precious book, now I daily read it and do rejoice. I want to know more about your Christ and His people.

The other day I saw in my friend's house *The Greatest Is Love*. What a fine book you have produced. I would also like to possess it if it is of no inconvenience to you.

Only one letter among the hundreds arriving each week was not appreciated. Fortunately, a secretary at the New Delhi office was suspicious and quickly dipped it in water. It was addressed to Ro, and it contained a bomb.

They passed the 300,000 mark in India. With 900,000 to go, Ro was looking beyond his own country. In the monthly newsletter and promotional mailings he listed other Asian countries and the number of telephones in each: Nepal 6,200, Burma 162,000, Thailand 152,000, Ceylon (Sri Lanka) 62,000, Sikkim 250, and so on. He hoped that churches, clubs, and cities might sponsor certain countries of their choice.

The Rev. Lud Golz, a pastor in Novelty, Ohio, saw the figures and asked his family if they would like to take little Sikkim with 250 telephones as their Christmas present to the Lord. The children looked up information about the small state in their encyclopedia: population 200,000, Buddhist and Hindu; no Christian churches. They prayed and told the Lord they were willing to sacrifice some presents so that the leaders of Sikkim might receive the New Testament.

It was set up so the Golzes could handle the project completely. Mother and Father typed the addresses, and the four children helped pack and apply labels and stamps. Even five-year-old Jess had a part.

After delivering the Bibles to the post office, they prayed that the Lord would use them. The children's prayers

ranged from "Bless Sikkim as they get the Bibles" to peti-
tions like "Lord, get the Bibles to Sikkim safely and
quickly" and "Give the people a desire to read the Bible,
and may some come to know you."

While suspensefully awaiting hoped-for responses to arrive, they were jolted by news of an attempted revolution
and fighting in the streets of Sikkim's capital. "Lord, protect the Bibles," they prayed. "Let people read them and
find peace."

The first letter came a few days later:

> My friend and I returned home from fighting and
> found a package on the doorstep. It was the Bible you
> sent. We read it with great interest. The next day we
> did not demonstrate against the government.

When it became evident that they were going to complete the mailing to India before the year was up, Ro and
Mawii decided to see firsthand just how the New Testaments were being received.

They landed in New Delhi to find the press very curious
about the thousands of colorful Testaments being mailed
into India. Many newsmen came to this, their first press
conference, representing the *India Express, Hindustan
Times,* and other leading newspapers. They asked keen
to-the-point questions and listened courteously to Ro's
answers.

The next day the articles came out. To Ro's amazement
every one of them was friendly. It was an exciting contrast
to a recent flurry of publicity over the expulsion of a
missionary.

One reporter came back and told Ro and Mawii of an interesting interchange he had had with his editor over the
story.

" 'Why did you write a missionary story like this?" my
editor asked me.

" 'Read it,' I told him.

" 'No,' he said. 'I don't want to read a missionary story.'
" 'Then why did you send me out?' I replied. 'If you can't at least read what I write I don't want to work for you any longer.'

"Then he read it and smiled. 'This man is different and what he is doing is different. I'll print it.' "

Sensing the great interest in New Delhi, Ro decided to try an experiment. He rented a well-known auditorium, seating 650, called the Sapru House, and placed ads in the capital's two leading newspapers. The announcements invited those receiving *Living New Testaments* to come the following evening at seven and "hear the life story of the man who sent you this book."

"I wonder what the response will be," Ro mused to Mawii as he paced up and down in their hotel room. "What if no one comes? This should have been planned well in advance. Why didn't I think of it earlier?"

An hour and a half before the meeting was to begin, the auditorium manager called with overwhelming news. "The building is already packed! We're turning people away. Please come over now; we don't know what to do with all these people."

Ro's voice had been bothering him, but they hurried over. He quickly took charge. First he introduced his beautiful Mawii, who gave a brief testimony. Next he spoke for forty to fifty minutes, telling what the Lord had done for him and his tribe. Then his voice began to tire.

"I cannot speak any longer," he said huskily, "but if those who want to talk to us further about believing in Jesus Christ will come to the front, we will try to help you."

About half the audience tried to crowd forward, but it was impossible for anyone to move more than a few feet. Ro returned to the speaker's stand. "My friends, there are so many wanting to come, it is impossible to see you all. Could you please call my office tomorrow instead?

"It has been a pleasure sharing with you. If there is anything I can do to bring you joy and peace, let me know. We are willing and ready to help you. May God be with you."

The next day the phone rang continuously. Ro and Mawii were ecstatic as they witnessed to the many inquirers. "Surely, this is all the evidence we need that God is behind this idea," Ro said. "He is blessing and using his Word in a greater way than I ever dreamed possible."

Even on the plane to Imphal, where they were going to have another meeting, they had opportunities to share Christ.

"Ro, the whole atmosphere seems so charged with the power of the Spirit of God, witnessing seems just as natural as breathing!" Mawii exclaimed.

When they stepped out of the airplane, the first to greet them was Ro's father, Chawnga. As they embraced in welcome, he asked, "How is it coming, my son? The Bible distribution."

"God has done great things. We will soon see the completion of India."

"All India! You have gone that far?" Chawnga exclaimed, surprised and amazed.

"Yes, God has been blessing and we have gone that far. But even more important, my father! We have just come from meeting with many who received the Book. They are hungry for more. I never expected to see so much spiritual enthusiasm in India. The Sapru House was packed to overflowing."

"I didn't know that Hindu Indians would be that interested."

"Nor did I. But that is what is so exciting! It works, my father. It really works! Bible distribution is the key to reaching men for Christ. We can reach the world for Christ through the Word. I am fully convinced of it."

Tears welled up in the wise old man's eyes. "My son, God has truly opened to you a great horizon!"

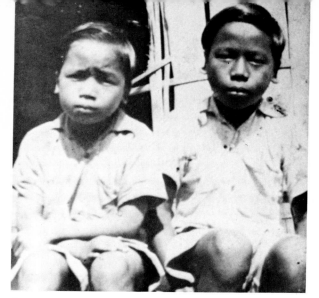

*Ro at the age of seven with his brother Ramlien,
posing for their father in their Sunday best.*

*Ro wore a borrowed coat to
have his high school picture
taken . . .*

*. . . and, ten years later, a
Nehru jacket.*

Ro and Mawii on their wedding day, January 1, 1959.

*Standing with Watkin Roberts, "Mr. Young Man,"
soon after Ro started the mission.*

The first graduation class at Sielmat Christian High School, 1962.

Below: Hmar girls at work in the school library in 1971.

Ro's brother Ramlien (far right) dedicates a new church in Binakhandi village.

Below: Ro visits with President V. V. Giri of India in the Presidential Palace in January, 1973.

Ro and Mawii mail the millionth copy of The Greatest Is Love.

This letter was sent to Ro from India and reached him in Wheaton, Illinois, without any address at all.

The Pudaite family: Johnny, Mary, and Paul Pudaite stand
(from left to right) in front of their parents and their grandfather, Chawnga.

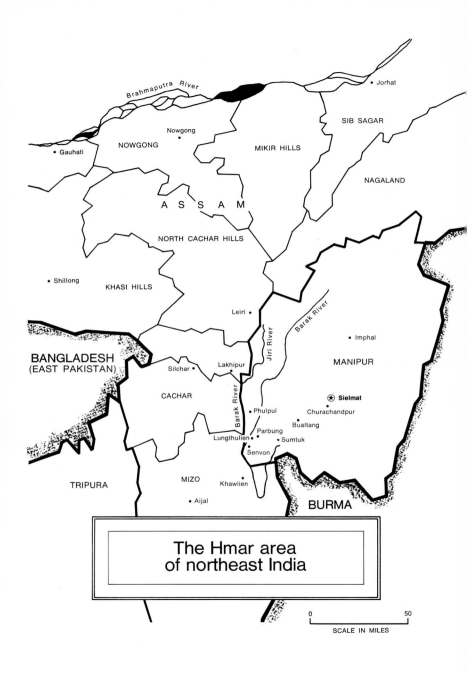

Brahmaputra River

• Jorhat

SIB SAGAR

Nowgong
•

NOWGONG

MIKIR HILLS

• Gauhati

NAGALAND

A S S A M

NORTH CACHAR HILLS

• Shillong

KHASI HILLS

Leiri •

Barak River

• Imphal

Jiri River

BANGLADESH
(EAST PAKISTAN)

Silchar •

Lakhipur •

MANIPUR

CACHAR

Barak River

⊛ Sielmat

Churachandpur
•

• Phulpui

Bualtang
•

Parbung
•

Lungthulien •

• Sumtuk

Senvon •

TRIPURA

MIZO

Khawlien
•

BURMA

• Aijal

The Hmar area
of northeast India

0   50

SCALE IN MILES